Hope you enjoy your day and the book! All the best [signature]

Rugby's First Pro

ROB ANDREW MBE

World Cup '95 Diary

Independent UK Sports Publications

COVER PHOTOGRAPHY

Front Page clockwise: Rob Andrew celebrates after scoring a last minute drop goal to put Australia out of the competition; the one that got away - All Blacks phenomenon Jonah Lomu escapes a Rob Andrew flying tackle in the semi-final defeat by New Zealand; Sprinboks' captain Francois Pienaar lifts the Webb Ellis Trophy to send the whole of South Africa into a frenzy; the England players relax in the Durban surf.

Back Page: Rob Andrew pictured with his four-year-old daughter Emily after receiving his MBE at Buckingham Palace shortly after returning from South Africa; the Aussies try in vain to force down the Rob Andrew drop goal that put them out of the 1995 World Cup; Rob Andrew pictured on the day he became Director of Rugby Development at Newcastle.

Photos by: Colorsport, Press Association, Express Newspapers, Empics and Rob Andrew.

First published in Great Britain 1995 by Independent UK Sports Publications
7-9 Rathbone Street, London W1P 1AF
Telephone 0171-636-5599

Text Copyright © Rob Andrew 1995
Design Copyright Independent UK Sports Publications 1995

ISBN 1-899429-04-2

Edited by Philip Evans

Printed by The Polar Print Group
2 Uxbridge Road, Leicester LE4 7ST
Telephone 0116 - 261 0800

Rugby's First Pro

ROB ANDREW MBE

World Cup '95 Diary

Dedicated to Sara, Emily and Beth

ACKNOWLEDGEMENTS: Thanks to all the England players, management and coaches for the intrusion into their precious leisure time on tour. My thanks also to Philip Evans and Mark O'Conor at Independent UK Sports Publications, the publishers, and Simon Pearson at The Polar Print Group.

Rugby will never be the same

Dateline: Monday, October 2nd 1995
Kingston Park, Newcastle.

Here I am sat at my new desk at Kingston Park, as rugby union's first full-time professional in the newly-created role of Director of Rugby Development for the Newcastle United Sporting Club. So much has happened in such a short time since the England squad returned from South Africa, disappointed that yet again the Southern Hemisphere countries had triumphed in another World Cup. This is my record of our ill-fated bid for glory - but as a prelude to my World Cup 95 Diary, I offer my views on the game we love so much going professional. When we arrived back at Heathrow on Monday, June 26th, we all knew the game had to change dramatically, but none us - me included - could have predicted such a tumultuous few weeks. Rugby Union will never be the same.

The drive to professionalism has been well documented - not least in the chapters you are about to read - and before the 1995 World Cup, many in the Southern Hemisphere felt it was the only way the game could go. Following on from the World Cup, the biggest move in this direction was a proposal to set up a Rugby World Conference and this was even discussed by the players at the World Cup dinner. This was supposedly backed by Kerry Packer with a view to creating a professional rugby circus above the current structure, attempting to sign 900 of the world's best players, competing in northern, central and southern conferences on the lines of American football. This would have taken the game completely professional, with the control being snatched from the hands of the governing unions. In essence, this was only stopped from happening by the Southern Hemisphere unions of Australia, New Zealand and South Africa offering to pay their players similar amounts of money, financed by Rupert Murdoch through a ten-year television deal.

Obviously, things were hotting up and the August meeting of the International Rugby Football Board in Paris took on even greater significance. No one in their wildest dreams felt the International Board would go as far as proclaiming the game open and professional - but this is exactly what they did. The working party dealing with amateurism - or shamateurism - had been chaired by Vernon Pugh QC, a member of the Welsh committee with an astute legal brain who had managed to persuade the International Board that this was the right decision. I think everybody thought they would fudge the issue once more and try to keep the game amateur while removing all the restrictions which prevented players earning from "rugby related" activities, although how anybody defined this was more and more open to dispute. So the bomshell was dropped just as everyone expected another fudge and further postponement. But here we were suddenly faced with all restrictions being lifted from the game, a course of action pushed for by the South Hemisphere unions who would have ignored any other ruling by the International Board. Some of the other unions, most notably Argentina and Ireland, were arguing for the retention of amateurism.

In the end it was the wisest decision they could have taken for the integrity and honesty of rugby union. We all knew the rules on amateurism had been flouted for many years all around the world, so why not come clean and let market forces dictate just how far professionalism would penetrate the game. Although there were some outcries that this would ruin the sport, I tend to disagree. There will be two or three years of settling down, but in the long run it will be the best move the game has ever made, and purely from a playing point of view it is totally necessary as far the Northern Hemisphere is concerned to compete with our friends in the Southern Hemisphere. They have already gone professional on the field. The only way we can catch up is allow our future players to be professional off the field so that they will have a chance on the field. Cries of "this will bankrupt our club" are, I believe, a total misunderstanding of the situation. Like many other sports, professionalism will find its level at the top end and for 90 per cent of players and administrators in this country it will have limited effect. It is only the elite few at the top who will be able to earn a living from rugby. Professionalism has never affected my enjoyment of tennis, golf and cricket in which the

top participants make a living and I don't. Why should it be any different in rugby?

Although this threw the home nations into mild panic, with no guide lines being left in which to operate in a professional world, the clean start will better the game. The RFU have accepted that rugby at international level will go professional with contracts this year for England players to earn between £30,000 and £40,000 per annum. They have restricted any payments to players below international level while they commission reports on the whole of the professionalism issue, and this seems to be somewhat of a delaying tactic. Once the game has gone professional, surely it is impossible to stop it?

The door has now been opened for the entrepreneurs to enter what they perceive to be

There's an awful lot to live up to at Newcastle. Sir John Hall and Kevin Keegan have achieved miracles in such a short time - and I'm planning to do the same on the rugby side.

new business opportunities. Within a flash Sir John Hall, the Chairman of Newcastle United Football Club, entered discussions with Newcastle Gosforth Rugby Club, the struggling Second Division side, with a view to it being part of his sporting empire in Newcastle. Within two weeks the deal had been struck and the day after this was announced I was approached by two Newcastle United directors, Douglas Hall, Sir John's son, and vice-chairman Freddie Shepherd. We had met within 24 hours and after a week of negotiations I signed a deal to become the new Director of Rugby Development for Newcastle United Sporting Club. My brief is to develop the game in the North of England, particularly the North East, from schoolboy level right through to the seniors at Gosforth, to be renamed

Here I am on the hallowed turf of St James' on the day I signed for Newcastle.

Newcastle Rugby Football Club, with the aim to take the club into the First Division as soon as possible to become a leading force in rugby in this country and in Europe.

It all happened extremely quickly and this demonstrates the power of the professional world rugby union is now entering. It also emphasises the vision of Sir John Hall to create the Newcastle United Sporting Club as an umbrella for other sporting activities, including a centre of excellence in Newcastle.

It would be an understatement to say how excited I am about the future, although I am facing a daunting and challenging task. It's just amazing how quickly rugby has moved in the last few months - further than in the last 100 years put together. I am totally confident about the future of the game and do not feel that professionalism will be detrimental to the sport I love. There will be changes but in the long run they will be for the better of the game and will help to attract more youngsters to a growing sport that I hope to be part of for a long time to come.

The last few months of my life have passed in a flash. We prepared well for a World Cup we thought we could win, only to be hit by the farce of the Will Carling affair. Player power won the day and off we went to South Africa full of confidence. In truth, we never really got going, although we had our moments. We experienced the highs and lows of international rugby in a few short weeks - our emotions were stretched to the limit with that last minute, breathtaking victory over Australia. Then we had our guts ripped out by Jonah Lomu and the All Blacks and we had to sit back and watch the fairytale scenes of South Africa winning their first World Cup on home soil. Along the way I was awarded the MBE. And now I face the biggest challenge of my rugby career in the sporting hothouse of the North East.

So much has happened in such a short time that the days when I recorded this Diary serve as a permanent reminder that rugby union the World Cup will never be the same again.

World Cup '95

by Richard Bath,
Editor, RUGBY NEWS

It was 5.45 in the morning and I'd been awake for the past 12 hours listening to the sound of London-bound South African fans celebrating their World Cup win. The big, bearded Afrikaner civil engineer in the seat next to me hadn't shown any inclination to talk to me for the previous few hours, but by now, as the plane circled over Heathrow, he was in an alcohol-induced goodwill-to-all-men mood and leant over, motioning to me to listen to a couple of words of South African wisdom.

"You are English?" he asked. I nodded. A big grin spread over his face. "So, how was it for you?" he asked, smiling. "Tell me, what will you remember of South Africa?"

A whole welter of images came back to me. Long nights in Cape Town, soaking wet days in Durban, Rob Andrew's momentous drop-goal against Australia and the frenzied scenes that followed the Springboks' win over the All Blacks in that unbearably tense finale to the tournament. All were moments that, pieced together, produced one of the most tumultuous month's in the working life of any rugby journalist.

But it is never possible to completely divorce work from the rest of your life. And for me, as an Englishman, there is one image that sums up the World Cup. It is of Jonah Lomu, England's nemesis and the one-man freak show who dominated proceedings, brushing off Tony Underwood and Mike Catt to mark the beginning of the end for England.

Not only was that the moment which effectively marked the end of England's meaningful part in the proceedings – and the end of a couple of distinguished careers to boot – but it was the single defining score of the World Cup, a momentous try which started one of the most startling games in the short history of World Cups.

Sitting safe and well in the press box, it is very easy to come up with all sorts of theories on how to stop the rampaging All Black wing. Yet, a few days later as I was sitting in the Johannesburg sunshine waiting for the final to kick-off, I finally understood why they are all more or less flawed. Sitting there in front of me was Jonah's Mum. To call her expansive would be a laughable understatement; her vast bulk took up two and a half seats, and the thought of one of her offspring moving towards Tony Underwood at the same rate as a charging rhino gave me a unique insight into the poor Leicester winger's plight.

But if the English train came off the tracks in spectacular style at the hands of Mr Lomu & Co, the signs that England were not functioning effectively were there for all to see from the moment that they ran out to face Argentina at King's Park, Durban, in their first game of the tournament. Dean Richards may have been missing, but with that admittedly mighty exception, England were at full strength – even if it barely showed. The last time these two sides met, England walked away with it, winning 51-0 at Twickenham. While no one expected a re-run of that mis-match, even fewer expected Argentina to put England under the sort of pressure they experienced. With the Pumas front five dominant at the set-piece – especially, and predictably, on Victor Ubogu's side of the scrum – England failed to establish any real continuity and were forced to rely on Rob Andrew's boot again.

Save for that, England's main emotion in the immediate aftermath of the game was of relief that neither of the Argentine kickers, Lisandru Arbizu and Ricardo Crexell, were able to convert any of the Pumas pressure. Otherwise, the Pumas would probably have secured a famously unlikely victory.

Although Arbizu's late try made the scoreline look artificially close, it had been an inauspicious start for a side which was widely perceived as one of the top four sides in the tournament. Andrew's heightened kicking consistency – for which Dave Alred gets a big round of applause – saw England right, but the weaknesses at the set-piece and in midfield going forward were too glaring to be easily glossed over. Worse still, while they were as deferential as ever on the record, in off the record briefings the Italians and Western Samoans, the remaining two pool opponents, were convinced that England had yet to come to terms with the task ahead. In the toughest of pools, any hint of weakness or of unexpected points now available ensured that the remainder of England's journey to the quarter-finals would be anything but smooth.

Italy were next in line, and faced England at King's Park six days after the tournament had kicked off, and just four days after their unimpressive win over the Pumas. The Italians were improving rapidly, and had come closer than any other side to beating Australia in the 12 months before the World Cup in South Africa. And not only had they come within a whisker of winning two Tests Down Under, but they had also beaten a full-strength Ireland side by 22-12 less than a month before the tournament got underway. No pushovers these Azzurri.

Even so, the overwhelming anticipation was that England would dispatch the Italians with relative ease, especially given the unfavourable media write-ups the lacklustre win over Argentina had produced. Yet nothing could be further from the truth, despite the fact that there were certainly good points in the England win. Centre Phil de Glanville, for instance, had an outstanding game, as did debutant starter at loosehead Graham Rowntree, while Rob Andrew continued his habit of keeping the scoreboard ticking over and England finally scored a try (embarrassingly, England were the last side in the tournament to register on the try-count, with even the hapless Ivory Coast back division beating the Five Nations champions to that status!).

Yet for every good point in England's win, there were frailties laid bare and limitations exposed. The Italians did well in all phases, and were able to survive primarily by forcing England into errors. Continuity wasn't on the Rosbifs' menu, and it was the exponents of "Spaghetti Rugby" who impressed. With prop Massimo Cuttitta and full-back Paolo Vaccari matching tries from Rory Underwood and brother Tony, England were again forced to rely on captain for the day Andrew's kicking – five penalties and a conversion to go alongside six penalties and two drop-goals in the 24-18 win over Argentina – to see them into the quarter-finals. Even then, Vaccari's late try made it an uncomfortably close shave, England going through by 27-20.

While England's last match produced their finest performance, as they saw off Western Samoa 44-22, it was a game littered with errors ... and bodies. By the end of an ultra-physical encounter, both sides had used all four permissible replacements and a constant stream of casualties had given team physio Kevin Murphy the most rigorous 80 minutes of exercise in his life. England had made it into the quarter-finals, yet all was far from well judging from the evidence of the pools stage.

Elsewhere, the tournament had thrown up more than its fair share of talking points and memorable moments. In Pool One, the whole event had started in the best circumstances available as South Africa, the host nation, beat champions Australia in an earth-shattering occasion. Sheer will saw the Springboks through, and the effect of success was startling; not because of the impact it had on the white community, but because of the effect it had on black South Africa. Everywhere I went, there were black kids wearing t-shirts with Francois Pienaar's beaming face painted in the South African flag beaming out. And as if to reciprocate, the white community took the Causa anthem "Shosolomo" to their hearts, even if most didn't quite manage to make it past the first line. There are few times when sportsmen have the opportunity to achieve something with a far wider significance, yet it would not be going too far to say that the national team striving success did seem to act as a catalyst to social understanding, if not change. Only time will help us learn whether this was illusory or real.

Given the significance of success for the nation, the events in Boet Erasmus Stadium, Port Elizabeth, when the host side met Canada, were all the more surprising. The portents were not good when the floodlights broke down as the two sides lined up in the tunnel ready to walk onto the pitch, but things went steadily downhill once they were eventually turned back on 45 minutes later. The first half was reasonably quiet as the Springboks scored two pushover tries, but with just seven minutes remaining, the niggling tension that had pervaded the game boiled over as wings Pieter Hendriks and Winston Stanley engaged in some harmless handbagging, only to have Canadian full-back Scott Stewart steam in and unleash an on-field riot. In the ensuing melee, punches were thrown and players kicked and shoved as chaos reigned. By the time referee McHugh pulled the plug on an ugly scene, Canadian captain Gareth Rees, prop Rod Snow and Springbok hooker James Dalton had all done enough to warrant an early bath. Hendriks was also subsequently banned for his part.

Yet if the disgraceful scenes in Port Elizabeth were a low point in Pool One in which rugby played little part, the one of the high points of the pool came in the encounter between Australia and Romania. Although winning easily, the Lynagh-less Australians were having a spot of bother with their place-kicking. So, who should step forward – none other than 6ft 8in second row John Eales. Not only that, but to wild applause he stroked four consecutive conversions through the posts, three of them touchline conversions. Now, can you really see Martin Johnson beating that?

In an uneventful Pool Three, the main talking point was New Zealand's record 145-17 win over Japan, a win in which wing Marc Ellis set a record of six tries in a game. One London bookmaker predicted that the All Blacks would win by 55 points, and lost £5,000 every time a point was subsequently scored. An expensive afternoon's rugby!

The other consistent record-breaker in attendance at the tournament was Scotland's Gavin Hastings. Not content with notching up 44 points in the Scots opening game against the Ivory Coast, the full-back went on to score 31 points against Tonga and 14 against France. Even so, Hastings would have swapped all of those points for a win against the French which would have put Scotland into a quarter-final against Ireland. Instead, 79 minutes of gutsy endeavour in the game against France was not enough to stop wing Emile Ntamack, who dived over in the last movement of the game to give France a 22-19 win against the run of play.

Pool Four was also notable for an injury to 24-year-old Ivory Coast player Max Brito. Playing against Tonga, Brito fell awkwardly and broke his neck. He is now paralysed from the neck downwards and will remain a paraplegic for the rest of his life.

If the pool stages were a tasty hors d'oeuvre, then the quarter-finals were as fine a main course as the tens of thousands of travelling fans could have wished for. New Zealand unleashed the Jonah Roadshow against the Scots, France overwhelmed Ireland in an admittedly poor match and South Africa engaged in a wince-making bruising war of attrition with the Samoans.

Yet for all the quality on display in the other three quarter-finals, it was England's Cape Town clash with champions Australia which was to prove one of the matches of the tournament. It could never have been described as a classic feast of running rugby, yet as a sporting spectacle it was utterly compelling. Neither side managed to gain any significant advantage as Lynagh and Rob Andrew matched each other, penalty by penalty, with their kicking duel broken up by tries from Tony Underwood and Australia's Damian Smith.

With the scores tied at 22-22 and both sides becoming increasingly frenzied in their attempts to secure possession, the game looked odds-on to go to extra-time. It was then that Rob Andrew stepped in. Kicking wise, his had been a fine tournament to that date, but the drop-goal which won the game at the death was probably the finest moment in his long career.

The best way to describe that kick is to describe the reaction of a young man I continually bumped into in South Africa. Jason Ovens was a very promising schoolboy scrum-half until he was involved in an horrific car crash aged 17. The surgeons thought that the Bristolian would never walk again, and told him he would certainly never play rugby again. Five years on and still having difficulty walking, Jason derives his pleasure from watching others play the game and had followed England since Day One in South Africa. His verdict was emphatic: "That was one of the most amazing games I have ever seen. In fact it was one of the most amazing days of my life. To be present at something like that was just something I will never, ever forget. It makes all the trouble of coming out here completely worthwhile." Case rested.

Yet for England it proved to be a false dawn. As with France in 1987 when beating Australia took so much out of them, the challenge of rising to the occasion again within the space of a few days proved too much. Jonah Lomu took over, Josh Kronfeld followed in his wake and within seven minutes four years of English planning went down the pan. Heads dropped, the usually impeccable Andrew had a nightmarish afternoon and England were consigned to playing a virtually meaningless game against France for the right to say they came third.

Yet so shattered were England after the way in which they lost to New Zealand that they were unable to rise to that occasion either and ended up losing to the French – and losing well – for the first time since 1988. Not that the French were feeling much better about being in Pretoria rather than Johannesburg; they had left the sodden King's Park pitch in tears after controversially losing 19-15 to South Africa in a game played in an inch of water after a tropical rainstorm.

The manner of their win did not bother Kitch Christie's Springboks overmuch, though. As soon as they reached the final there was a tremendous outpouring of emotion, and a feeling that the hosts were fated to win the tournament. By the time the final got underway in a frenzy of national pride and an amazing pre-match show which featured a fly-pass by a jumbo jet, Johannesburg's Ellis Park was as tense as any stadium I have ever seen.

Nelson Mandela came to see "our boys" off, while the whole of South Africa was willing Pienaar's men on, willing the Boks to bury the Kiwi menace, Jonah Lomu. And if the final lacked a try, it lacked for little else as the tensest of games went to extra-time. Helped along by repeated taped renditions of the South African national anthem throughout the game – not to mention the

fact that the game was played at altitude shortly after the bulk of the All Blacks mysteriously contracted food poisoning – the Springboks eventually won through courtesy of a last-minute drop-goal from fly-half Joel Stransky.

I can honestly say that I have never seen a mass outpouring of spontaneous emotion on the scale that greeted the final whistle that confirmed South Africa's win. The country went absolutely ballistic, as horns sounded nonstop throughout the night and Johannesburg was drunk dry. Even as long after as two days later, South Africa seemed to be in a state of collective delirium, and on the night I vividly remember the drive away from the stadium. So hyped up were the South African fans that the road heading into the city looked like a war zone. Cars littered the whole area, and ambulances milled around, tending to those South Africans who had fallen from their precarious perches on the back of pick-up trucks.

That night, though, just five hours after the final, an incident occurred which put everything into perspective. Drinking in a bar, I spotted the completely bald head of All Black Josh Kronfeld. Absolutely amazed that he should be out so soon after the biggest game of his life, I wandered over and said hello. Wasn't he physically and mentally drained, I asked, and didn't he just want to relax. "No," he said. "After all, at the end of the day it's just a game of football and you have to remember that." With that he went back to his pint, and I chewed on that food for thought.

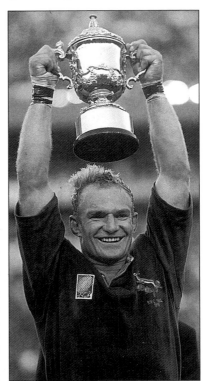

Francois Pienaar, South Africa captain, holds the Webb Ellis Trophy aloft.

**Rob gives the low-down on his World
Cup playing colleagues and coaches**

The England
World Cup Squad

WILL CARLING.

Born in Bradford-upon-Avon, Will was educated at Sedborough School and Durham University. His senior rugby career started at Durham University and he first represented the North in the Divisional Championship in 1987. He continued to play for the North despite having no residence or birth qualification when he moved to London, and after brief spells with the Army and Mobil Oil he set up his own marketing and motivational company - Insights Limited. Known as the Skipper, he is the most successful international rugby captain of all time and has only missed two England internationals in the whole of his career.

JONATHAN CALLARD

Affectionately known as 'JC' in the squad, he spent his early career in Wales for Newport before moving over to Bath to pursue a career with England. He was successful in this following the retirement of John Webb, and 'JC' will always be remembered for his last minute penalty to beat Scotland at Murrayfield in 1994.

MIKE CATT

'Catty' was born in Port Elizabeth in South Africa and came to England in 1992 to visit an uncle in Stroud. Having tried to contact Gloucester to see if he could get a game, he turned his attention to Bath where they soon realised they had a talent on their hands. In Jeremy Guscott's absence, he partnered Phil de Glanville in the centre, and last season after the retirement of Stewart Barnes, played fly-half. He came into the England side as a replacement for Paul Hull against Canada and has never looked back.

IAN HUNTER

'Hunts' was born in Harrow, although educated in the Lake District. Now playing for Northampton, he has suffered from injuries since his debut against Canada in 1992, and was also unfortunate to be injured in the opening game of the 1993 Lions tour to New Zealand against North Auckland, forcing him to return home. Other injuries last season prevented him from playing a great deal, although he fought his way back into the World Cup squad.

TONY UNDERWOOD

Born in Ipoh, Malaysia, Tony was educated with brother Rory at Barnard Castle School and then Cambridge University before working for Crosbie Securities in the City. One of the quickest players in the England squad and also one who takes most advantage of Austin Swaine, our psychologist (The Spook), to help him prepare for games.

RORY UNDERWOOD

Unlike brother Tony, Rory was born in the UK in Middlesbrough and I joined him at Barnard

Castle School at the age of 11. We were in the same boarding house and rugby and cricket teams for seven years. Now in the RAF, he is England's most capped player and leading try scorer of all time. He has even been on This Is Your Life!

JEREMY GUSCOTT

'Precious' as he is affectionately known, was a product of the Bath Mini's and is now a part-time Public Relations Officer with British Gas, part-time model and part-time TV personality. He was selected for the 1989 British Lions Tour to Australia before being capped by England, and then went on to score four tries in his debut against Romania, – a far cry from his early days as a bricky in Bath!

PHIL DE GLANVILLE

'De G' has been one of the unsung heroes of the successful Bath side for some time. He filled in very successfully for Jerry Guscott when Jerry was out for a year and has proved himself at the very highest level. He will be pushing hard this season for one of the centre positions when not attending committee meetings as Bath's new captain.

DAMIAN HOPLEY

'The Judge' was born in London and attended Harrow School where he was coached by Roger Utley. He then saw the light and studied Divinity at St Andrew's University before doing the one-year theology course at Cambridge University. Still not sure of his chosen vocation, he has spent the summer playing for Southland, in New Zealand, trying to spread the word in Invercargil.

DEWI MORRIS

The 'Welsh Monkey' was born in Crickhowel and educated at Alsagar College, Crewe, before starting his senior rugby career with Winnington Park and Liverpool St. Helens. He made his England debut in 1988 against the Australians following a successful campaign for the North side while still playing for Winnington Park. Dewi fought his way back brilliantly during the World Cup and always gives 100 per cent.

KYRAN BRACKEN

Kyran or 'Village' to his mates, is another one of the England exiles. Having been born in Dublin, he now plays for Bristol and has come through the ranks of the England under 16,18 and students into the senior side, making his debut in the famous victory over New Zealand in 1993 despite suffering a serious ankle injury in the first minute following a stamping by Jamie Joseph. He is now training to be a lawyer in Bristol. He's a player with a great future for England.

JASON LEONARD

'The Barking Chippy' or 'Golden Bollocks' moved from Saracens to Harlequins to improve his England selection hopes. He went on the tour to Argentina in 1990 before becoming established in 1991 as the successor to Paul Rendell and has never been out of the side since. With his Cockney sense of humour, he's one of the strong men of the squad and has recovered from a serious neck injury which required surgery to continue a very successful England career.

GRAHAM ROWNTREE

'Wiggy' or 'Yum Yum' after his hair style or his surname take your pick, he has come through the Leicester Academy following Dean Richards and Martin Johnson as a player with potentially a great England future. An Insurance Broker with P & G Bland in Leicester, he is one of the Leicester trio of intrepid front row forwards.

BRIAN MOORE

The 'Pitbull' is renowned for his fiercely competitive nature, both on and off the field, which has occasionally landed him in hot water. A long and distinguished England career going back to 1987 when he replaced Graham Dawe – their competition has continued ever since apart from a couple of performances by John Olver in the early 1990s, – Brian has been an ever-present following his early career at Nottingham before moving to Harlequins to follow in Jason's footsteps. A litigation partner with Edward Lewis & Co in London, he delights in his prosecution role at the team court.

GRAHAM DAWE

'Dawsey' has been around longer than anyone and is still one of the fittest members of the squad at the age of 36. He also travels the furthest for training with Bath from his farm in Launceston, being a three hours each way drive, just for training, not to mention all the extra sessions at Marlow for England just before the World Cup. He probably made a bundle on expense claims but is one of the most dedicated members of the squad.

VICTOR UBOGU

'Dadda' was born in Nigeria and spent his early senior career at Oxford University, Richmond and Mosley before finally deciding to play for Bath in spite of living in London. He made his England debut against Canada in 1992 and fought hard to replace the undoubted scrummaging ability of Jeff Probin to become established in the England side, a powerful runner when not involved in too much tight play. His business career has been extended with the pre-World Cup opening of Shoeless Joe's on the Kings Road, otherwise christened 'Beerless Joe's' by the squad following our visit prior to our trip to South Africa.

JOHN MALLETT

'Shep' was born in Lincoln in 1970 and is a student at Bath University where he plays his senior rugby alternating with Victor for the tighthead spot. Shep had a very good tour of South Africa last year and is another one of the young England players with a very good future ahead of him.

MARTIN JOHNSON

'Johners' came through the England schoolboy ranks before spending a season in New Zealand when he was capped for New Zealand Colts against Australia Colts. Had he stayed, he could have become a full All Black. He returned to the Midlands where he was one of the stalwarts of the Leicester Tigers team and made his international debut against France in 1990, following an injury to Wade Dooley on the eve of the Test. He also joined the 1993 Lions Squad as a replacement when Wade Dooley flew home, and has become one of the world's best second row forwards.

MARTIN BAYFIELD

'Bayf' is a policeman in the Bedfordshire Constabulary, having spent some time in the Met. He also played for Bedford before joining Northampton whom he helped down to the Second Division last season. Since winning his first caps in 1991 against Fiji and Australia, he has become one of the leading middle of the line second-row jumpers despite a serious neck injury, also suffered in New Zealand in 1993 on the Lions' Tour. He will be hoping to help Northampton to return to the First Division this season.

BEN CLARKE

'Clarkey' was born in Bishop's Stortford and was educated at the Royal Agricultural College, Cirencester, while still playing at Saracens. He was part of the exodus from Saracens and moved to Bath, making his international debut in 1993 before going on the British Lions Tour to New Zealand where he was rated by the All Blacks as one of the world's leading back-row forwards. He is now one of the new breed of part-time international rugby players, as well as being a part-time Promotions Executive for National Power. Good work if you can get it!

NEIL BACK

'Backy' was born in Coventry in 1969 and now plays his club rugby for Leicester alongside Dean Richards in the back row. His unmistakable shock of blond hair reminds everybody of the great Jean-Pierre Reeve of France. Backy made his international debut in 1994 against Scotland and has often made outstanding contributions to Barbarian matches where their style suits his own speed and ball skills.

TIM RODBER

Born in Richmond, Yorkshire, 'Rodders' is an officer in the Green Howards and unfortunately had the distinction of captaining Northampton down to the Second Division last season. He made his international debut in 1992 against Scotland in place of the injured Dean Richards, who subsequently replaced Tim during the game. He has been one of the stars of the England back row with Ben Clarke and Dean Richards for the last 18 months, particularly against New Zealand in 1993 and South Africa in the first test last year. Unfortunately, he also holds the distinction of being only the second Englishman to be sent off in international rugby in the match against Eastern Province on the tour of South Africa last summer.

STEVE OJOMOH

Another Nigerian in the England squad who was nearly deported from the country several years ago and only stayed through intervention at a high level from the Home Office. He currently plays his club rugby for Bath where he often spends much of the season in the second team in the shadow of John Hall. Made his international debut for England in 1994 and had an outstanding tour of South Africa last year to keep the pressure on the established back row forwards.

DEAN RICHARDS

Born in Warwickshire in 1963 and a stalwart of the Leicester club, the chant of 'Deano, Deano' is renowned the world over. He made his international debut in 1986 against Ireland and he scored two push-over tries. Despite occasionally being left out of the England side, he has nearly always fought his way back, and has been on two Lions Tours in 1989 and 1993. He is one of England's all-time great forwards.

THE MANAGEMENT

THE MANAGER/COACH: JACK ROWELL

One of the leading and most successful coaches in England club history with spells at Newcastle Gosforth and 17 years at Bath with unprecedented success in the 1980s. Took over the England job from Jeff Cook in 1994 and led England to the Grand Slam last season in his first Five Nations.

COACH: LES CUSWORTH

A long-time stalwart and servant of Leicester, along with Dusty Hare, who had an England playing career spanning the mid to late 1980s, one of the most inventive fly-halfs in English rugby and coach of the England Seven which won the World Sevens in 1993.

ASSISTANT MANAGER: JOHN ELLIOTT

A former Nottingham hooker, from whence came Brian Moore, and will be joining the RFU staff permanently from July as a Youth Officer with responsibility for bringing the Colts through to under 21 level and then onto senior international level.

COLIN HERRIDGE

'Mr Big' from Harlequins, a former Quins Secretary, now the Press Liaison Officer for the squad, charged with keeping reporters off our backs, although generally fails miserably He is not easy to talk to because he is always on his mobile phone organising golf for the Manager and Coach.

KEVIN MURPHY

'Smurf' is one of the leading physios in English rugby, having been with the team since the mid-1980s. He has also been on two Lions Tours in 1989 and 1993 and is highly regarded by all who have suffered at his hands. Likes a quiet beer when he has finished work of an evening.

DOCTOR TERRY CRYSTAL

A keen Yorkshire cricket follower and Leeds United fan, which explains some of his behaviour, keeps 'Smurf' company on some of his evenings out. He likes a good old sing-song when given the opportunity to get a microphone in his hand. Brufen and sleeping pills seem to be the remedy for everything!

DOCTOR AUSTIN SWAIN

The 'Spook' has come in useful for several members of the squad who need mental assistance, although after 12 months of working with this squad, I think he needs some assistance himself. He spent most of the World Cup spying on the opposition, being unceremoniously kicked out of one All Black training session.

REX HAZELDENE

A fitness instructor extrordinaire from Loughborough University, he makes himself very unpopular by forcing the boys to do (league) tests four times a year and does not allow any cheating. He works hard on fitness schedules for everybody, although I wonder how many are actually used properly.

DAVE ALRED

Despite some reluctance from Twickenham for him to join us on the trip, the kicking guru from Bristol, who also played Rugby League and American Football, was finally allowed to join us and even managed to get some of the other backs to improve their kicking. Onto the forwards next!

48 hours of pure farce

AQuestion of Sport for the year 2015: Which rugby team went to the 1995 World Cup without a captain? That was very nearly the position facing the England Rugby Union squad for the third ever Rugby World Cup to be held in South Africa, beginning May 26th .

On the morning of Saturday, May 6th, the day of the Pilkington Cup Final between Wasps and Bath, the officers of the Rugby Football Union made a press statement announcing that Will Carling would no longer be the England rugby captain. Will had been sacked at a meeting the previous Friday afternoon, at the East India Club, following remarks he made on a Channel Four documentary, first shown on the Thursday evening. Off camera, Will was heard to record that if the game was professional in England, would it need to be run by "57 old farts".

In fact, it subsequently transpired that the Rugby Football Union committee only comprises 56 members, not 57, and indeed six of these representing the senior officers, being the immediate past President, President and two senior Vice-Presidents, Treasurer and Assistant Treasurer, had decided along with Dudley Wood, the outgoing Secretary, that this was too much. Will no longer had the confidence of the officers of the Union and, in their view, was not fit to captain the England rugby team in South Africa, nor indeed to represent English sport in such a prestigious event.

The following 24 hours in particular, and in total 48 hours, were to prove a complete farce in the history of English rugby. The officers of the Union had completely misread the mood of the England squad, the public and indeed the press in England and cannot have possibly considered in enough detail the consequences of making such a momentous decision merely 10 days before England, one of the favourites for the competition, were to leave the shores of the United Kingdom to embark on what is now a major world sporting event.

Not only was the decision to sack Will proven to be a major mistake, but the timing, on the morning of the most important club rugby match of the season, the Pilkington Cup Final, did not go down too well with the sponsors of the competition, Pilkington themselves.

It was akin to the Football Association announcing the sacking of Terry Venables on the morning of the FA Cup Final and hoping there would be no reaction, that life would carry on as normal, and all that would be needed was the appointment of another captain to take over the reins and everybody would be happy.

Clearly, when you have a captain of Will Carling's stature, who has led the side for seven years and is now the most successful captain of international rugby ever in the history of the game, the catastrophic nature of that decision can be viewed for what is was.

I heard the decision as I was about to leave the Petersham Hotel in Richmond, the home of the England team before internationals and also on this occasion the home of the Wasps in preparation for the cup final against Bath. This obviously took the edge off the final as far as I was concerned and indeed, on arriving at Twickenham three quarters of an hour later, the media and the spectators were talking of nothing other than Will's sacking, which had just been publicly announced. I was later to find out that the car park was awash also with the controversy and the announcement had taken the edge off the day for the majority of spectators who had arrived on a glorious Spring day, with temperatures in the mid-20s, to enjoy a great game of rugby, only to spend most of the time discussing what would happen to Will Carling.

In the event, the final was an excellent game of rugby, although the result for Wasps went the wrong way with Bath coming out comfortable 36-16 winners. Again, after the final, all topics of conversation as far as the media were concerned were on the reactions by the England members on duty that day, namely myself and several of the Bath players. I decided the best course of action was not to comment on the decision until I was able to find out a little bit more about what was going on. I wanted to talk to Will before making any public statements. Some of my England colleagues in the Bath team, however, were not so reticent in coming forward and it became clear that there was a militant attitude within the squad. The players were very strongly behind Will and they were not going to take this decision lying down.

Several players were particularly scathing of the Rugby Football Union, including the Bath captain John Hall who said the England players should stand behind Will. Jon Callard was also quoted as saying that we would now see the strength of the England squad. After all, who was going to win the World Cup - the committee or the players? There was also a feeling from some insiders within the Union that a rash decision had been taken by a very small group without fully consulting the rest of the committee. Questions were asked as to whether this was constitutionally acceptable, and even if it was, it was a hasty decision taken over what amounted to flippant remarks off camera.

Clearly, a decision of this magnitude, after a very successful season in preparation for the World Cup, proved to the players beyond all reasonable doubt that certain members of the Rugby Union were not in the slightest bit interested in the success of the England team in the World Cup, but were far more interested in their own self importance. There was even a suggestion that some of the officers had been waiting for this moment for several years to get Will for what they perceived to be his radical views on how the game should be run, particularly on the professionalism issue. Obviously, if this decision was to stick it would have very serious consequences for the England squad who were now in the final throes of their preparation for the World Cup. A disruption of this nature would make us the laughing stock of the rest of the rugby world, which in fact it did,

I spoke briefly with Jack Rowell, the England team manager, and Will Carling on the Saturday night. I wanted to find out what was actually going on and whether there was anything we could do to stop such a decision being upheld to prevent the destruction of all the preparations that had taken place. Neither Will nor Jack were really able to outline any action which could be taken because clearly Will was in a weak position, having been stripped of the captaincy, and Jack had been requested by the Rugby Football Union committee to put forward a name of a new contender for the captaincy. He told them he was not prepared to do this immediately, but would wish to discuss this with some of the senior players. It was clear though from the reaction of the press and the England players who had commented on the Saturday evening that this situation could not continue.

I was able to relax for the rest of the evening, trying to enjoy the dinner with my Wasps colleagues and their wives and girlfriends, albeit in rather difficult circumstances, having just lost a major chance to bring some silverware back to Sudbury after taking part in our first Pilkington Cup Final since 1987.

This Saturday evening proved to be the lull before the storm. The phone started to ring at 7.15 on the Sunday morning and I had my final telephone conversation on the subject of Will's dismissal at 10.15 that evening, having spent much of the intervening time on the phone. The drums were beating as far as the England squad were concerned and it soon became apparent that there would be nobody interested in taking on the captaincy. Ben Clarke has subsequently taken some stick from the squad following his ghost written piece in the Sunday Telegraph, which had been put together on the Saturday evening after the cup final, commenting briefly on Will's dismissal, saying it was disappointing but life would have to go on without Will. Although Ben did not expect to be offered the captaincy, if he was asked he would obviously accept. You can imagine the England dressing room has not missed the opportunity to point out that Ben was the only one who went public on saying he would accept the England captaincy!

Dean Richards and I had been put forward as leading contenders following Will's sacking, although nobody

The uneasy truce: Will Carling and Dennis Easby, President of the RFU, shake hands after Will's reinstatement as captain.

was in fact asked by Jack Rowell to take on the job. By mid-morning on the Sunday both Dean and myself had gone public in saying that we would not be prepared to accept the captaincy in such circumstances. Dean and I had spoken to the majority of the World Cup squad and it became clear we would either go to South Africa without a captain or Will would have to be reinstated.

As we were making this collective decision, Dennis Easby, the President of the RFU who had ultimately taken the decision to sack Will, was going public and saying there was no way the situation could be reversed. He copped a huge amount of criticism in the press on the Sunday morning, in both the tabloids and broadsheets, to a degree which was so scathing that they had obviously underestimated the feelings of the country. It had been shown once and for all that the committee men who had taken this decision were totally out of touch with the game and its following. The sport was no longer purely in the domain of the rugby fraternity (where many of the committee would like to keep it) but was now very much in the eyes of the whole English public. Will was receiving support from all sectors. In fact, many surveys showed that more than 95 per cent of those questioned thought Will should be reinstated. By mid-afternoon we felt that the RFU could do nothing but return the captaincy to Will. In fact, his agent, Jon Holmes, was able to talk to Dennis Easby on UK Talk Radio mid-afternoon on Sunday and persuade Dennis that he ought to meet Will on the Monday to discuss the whole issue. He pointed out that in all of this Will had never been summoned to defend, or even discuss his comments, and neither had Jack Rowell been consulted on the impact the decision would have on the team.

To confirm the players' position we issued a brief press statement late on Sunday afternoon respectfully requesting the RFU to reconsider their decision and that the whole team stood behind Will. We were looking forward to this being resolved so that we could continue with our World Cup preparations. By the time the squad were to meet the next day at Marlow for one of our regular pre-World Cup training sessions the farce was over. Dennis Easby and Will Carling had met and made statements that there was regret on both sides for the comments made and that Will was to be reinstated as England captain for the period of the World Cup and this would be reconsidered by the committee on our return from South Africa.

We went out to training at Marlow that evening with Will back at the helm and were watched by a large group of supporters and the media circus following the story. In 48 hours the whole comedy of errors had come to a close. As Brian Moore was heard to say, the only thing missing was Brian Rix - and we were expecting him to appear at any moment!

What to the rest of the rugby world, if not the sporting world, would seem a complete aberration by the RFU committee, may well have far-reaching consequences for the future of the game in England and, indeed, future England rugby squads. This had been the first opportunity for an England squad to effectively flex their muscles and use the rather emotive term "player power". This is not something that rugby players are genuinely comfortable with, certainly not in the Northern Hemisphere, although perhaps more so in the Southern Hemisphere. We had had the odd opportunity over the last four or five years when the relations between the committee and the players had worsened significantly to flex our power, although we had never felt strong or confident enough to do this. However, on this occasion there was no doubt there was only one decision the players were prepared to take and this meant resisting the committee.

The conflict with our own Union has always surrounded the discussion on professionalism and what rewards players should be allowed, on and off the field, for playing international rugby. Over the last five years there have been significant advances made by the Southern Hemisphere to reward their players, particularly for off the field activities, monitored by the International Rugby Board, although many of these schemes in our eyes have sailed pretty close to the wind as far as the regulations are concerned. What the England squad had maintained since they started their players' promotions company in 1991 is that we would like to be treated by our Union in the same way as other unions around the world. We have not always felt we have had the same level of support for our efforts to make money from promotional activity. In the Southern Hemisphere it is clear that the players are working with the unions who in turn are very keen to help their players, particularly bearing in mind the threat from rugby league. In recent weeks this threat in both the Southern and Northern Hemispheres has increased significantly with the talk of the Super League being supported by Rupert Murdoch's News International Group once again putting huge amounts of money into the sport, thus being a serious threat to rugby union, especially in the Southern Hemisphere. Their unions will do all in their power to prevent players going across to rugby league and this will mean increased earnings for rugby union players which will in turn give them more time to devote to training and playing more high profile matches. We in the Northern Hemisphere must combat this threat in order that we ourselves can compete with our adversaries in Australia, New Zealand and South Africa.

I believe that the happenings of the of May 6th, 7th and 8th will have significant implications for the future of English rugby and in particular the relationships between the Union and the players which from this moment in time can only get better. They certainly can't get any worse. Having settled the issue of Will's captaincy we were able to turn our intentions to our opponents in South Africa.

Looking back, the events of those 48 hours were so crazy it was almost as if they really did not happen and everybody was having a bad dream.

How could the administrators have got it so wrong?

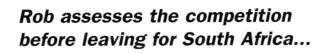

Rob assesses the competition before leaving for South Africa...

The Big Five

I have always felt there could be five possible winners of the 1995 World Cup - England, Australia, New Zealand, France or the hosts, South Africa. This, to my mind, makes the '95 World Cup by far the most interesting of the three so far held. In 1987 it was clear that the winner would only really come from Australia or New Zealand, albeit that France did make that final. In 1991 again Australia and New Zealand were the favourites and England were, perhaps, the surprise package of that tournament, reaching the final only to lose to Australia.

In those two World Cups South Africa were obviously absent and their readmittance into world sport has been a great tonic, particularly for rugby, where the game is huge in South Africa, and cricket. In both these sports they have thrown themselves back into the world scene with tremendous gusto and have taken on very difficult and torturous itineraries to get their players back up to speed in both games in which they excel and in which they have a claim on world dominance.

There are, of course, 11 other teams also taking part in the 1995 World Cup. My fear is that the majority of these are not anywhere near the same standards of the main five contenders and that we may see some fairly high scores as we did in the 1987 World Cup when there was a huge gap in playing ability between the top and bottom sides. Then there were some 50 and 60 point margins. These were closed in the 1991 competition as the majority of the emerging nations, such as Western Samoa, Fiji and Canada in particular, narrowed the gap on their big brother rivals. Some very good performances were put up by the Samoans and Canada only lost narrowly to New Zealand in the quarter final. In '95 I feel the top five have opened up this gap again, although I concede that Scotland could be added to this group, having defeated France in the 1995 Five Nations Championship after their disappointing 1994. The problem, as always for the Scots, will be to sustain this level of performance over a period of four or five weeks of high intensity. My view is that we will see some pretty high scores again and this is not necessarily good for the international game of rugby when all the power remains in a few select hands.

Coming back to the five leading contenders, there is considerable psychology in the build-up to the World Cup, with no one country wishing to take on the mantle of favourites and everybody making every other team their hot tip to take the pressure off themselves. We have had the Australians saying they fear England most, the English saying they rate the Aussies as the favourites, the South Africans keeping a low profile by their standards and the New Zealanders enjoying the relative obscurity of fourth or fifth favourites for the competition. This is a position they clearly like and one which, as we approach the start of the World Cup, the other nations are starting to put right. They have clearly had a disappointing 18 months by New Zealand standards, having lost to England, France and Australia. I would never right off a New Zealand team and although they have been going through a slight transition, particularly with the loss of Grant Fox, who was their main stay at fly-half for so long, they genuinely still have some of the best performers of the basic rugby skills in the world. I believe they will be one of the strongest teams in this competition. They have a very experienced pack of forwards led by Sean Fitzpatrick, aided by the reselection of prop Richard Loe, a second row containing Robin Brooke and Ian

Jones, who is one of the leading group of tall men dominating the middle of world line-outs, and a back row comprising Zinzan Brook and the rejuvenated Mike Brewer who missed the 1991 World Cup through injury. They have yet to find a consistent replacement for Grant Fox, although newcomer Andrew Mehrtens has just scored 28 points on his debut against Canada and may be one to watch for the competition. Frank Bunce and Walter Little are back in harness and although they have lost John Kerwood and John Timu to rugby league, I believe they have sufficient power and pace in the back line to cause most sides trouble. Jonah Lomu, 19 years old, 6ft 5 in and 17 stone, playing on the left wing, should be one to avoid!

The world champions Australia are once again firing on all cylinders and will be a major threat to any nation in the competition. Clearly their opening clash with South Africa will set the tone for the World Cup but will also have a significant bearing on who reaches the final four and half weeks later. Assuming England win their group, we will meet the losers of this match, who will no doubt be the runners-up in Pool A. The Australians are led by one of the best fly-halfs in the world, Michael Lynagh, and although his captain and half-back partner from 1991, Nick Farr-Jones, is missing, the back line still contains the mercurial David Campese, probably the best rugby player in the world as well as being the one with the biggest mouth! Joining him are Tim Horan and Jason Little, who have both recovered from very serious leg injuries. Little is back playing in the Australian side; Horan is waiting for his chance, although Daniel Herbert is doing a fine job replacing him and Tim may find it difficult to get back in the side. Lynagh is there to marshal them along with his new half-back partner George Gregan, a 21-year-old whose claim to fame in the Bledisloe Cup last year was a try saved in the last minute on New Zealand winger Jeff Wilson. His performance during this competition will be crucial to Australia and he may turn

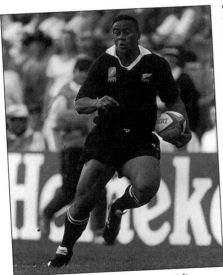

Jonah Lomu - one to avoid!

out to be a real star of the World Cup, or alternatively he may prove to be the one slight chink in the Aussie armour which teams at this level will exploit. Up front there is no real weakness in the Australian side with potentially the best front row in the world of Ewen McKenzie, Phil Kearns and Tony Daly, backed up by Rod McCall and John Eales in the second row. Eales will again play a big part in any Australian success and is arguably the best middle line-out forward in the world. The back row is very big and competitive and contains Tim Gavin, David Wilson and Willie Ofahengaue, who may not be the explosive figure he was in '91 but is still a formidable opponent. I expect Australia to have too much experience and class against the South Africans in the opening game, which will leave England probably playing South Africa in the quarter finals and Australia likely to proceed through the draw into the final on the June 24th, perhaps against England again?

The South Africans, although having a great number of very talented rugby players, do not appear to have settled on a consistent side, giving their players the chance to work together as a team over a long period. South African rugby selection is very political with a great deal of competition between the provinces. It appears that the province of the coach has a great bearing on the make up of the national squad and clearly Kitch Christie, the South African coach from Transvaal, has gone with many players from his province, which has been met with some disappointment in other parts of the country. They have quality players in nearly all positions, although do not yet appear to have settled on the best combinations. Their four half backs, Joost van der Westhuizen, Johan Roux, Hennie le

Roux and Joel Stransky, have all played tests in the last 18 months for South Africa without any-body emerging as the best player in his position. Andre Joubert at full-back could well become one of the stars of the World Cup but unfortunately Chester Williams, the only black member of the South African side, and a national hero, has had to withdraw from the team only days before the competition kicks off due to a hamstring injury. This is a big psychological blow to the South African team and one which will clearly not help their World Cup chances. Their for-wards, are, as always, big and aggressive and depend very much on the leadership qualities of Transvaal and Springbok captain Francois Pienaar. They will certainly be a very competitive and combative unit, especially on their own soil, and in Mark Andrews at second row, jumping at the front of the line-out, they have a world class forward who will certainly secure them some quality possession. However, being the host nation in such a prestigious and pressurised tour-nament, I feel sure that their ability to cope with the off-the-field pressures will play a very large part in the South African success or otherwise. Their lack of international experience may prove to be a difficult hurdle to overcome - although nobody should bet against them.

The French are, perhaps, the most difficult of the leading nations to read. Twelve months ago they were claimed as being one of the favourites for the World Cup following an historic 2-0 series victory over the All Blacks in New Zealand, which is no mean feat. They came back to the Northern Hemisphere with high hopes of winning a Grand Slam in the 1995 Five Nations and taking their success on to South Africa to win the World Cup. However, the only predictable thing about the French is their unpredictability, both on and off the field, and dur-ing 1995 they had a most disappointing Five Nations Championship, resulting in a heavy away defeat by England and a surprise defeat at the Parc des Princes by a Scottish team that had never won at that stadium. Still, they can never be written off and with the players of the qual-ity of Sella, Ntamack and Phillippe Saint Andre in the backs, and forwards of the ability of Roumat, Cecillon, Benetton, Cabannes and Benazzi, they will be a major force. I am not sure they have the mental ability to cope with a tournament of this intensity, although the draw has been quite kind to them, should they overcome Scotland in their group, probably leaving them with a semi-final meeting with Australia,

As for Scotland, they had an outstanding 1995 Five Nations and their clash with France will be very important, as the loser is likely to face New Zealand in the quarter-finals, a game which I cannot see Scotland winning. They could, however, upset France once again, which should also give them a very good chance of meeting Australia in the semi-final. And on their day, with Scotland anything can happen. They clearly have some very good players who have done it all before in Gavin Hastings, Craig Chalmers and the Scottish pack, which can range from the mediocre to the rampaging from game to game and even during a match. If they play with their usual fire and passion they could continue to upset the odds, although I do not believe they have the ability to withstand four or five highly pressurised games in such a short period and I expect France to beat them in their pool.

Ireland and Wales, who both had a disappointing Five Nations tournament, find themselves in the same group as New Zealand and Japan and although they should comfortably beat Japan, they will have to battle it out for the runners-up spot to have a date with the winners of Scotland or France in the quarter-final. I expect the limits of both team's aspirations to be a quarter-final berth and their clash in Pool C may not be a classic for the impartial fan, although for the avid Welsh or Irish supporter a one-point victory will suffice.

Pool A, or the group of death as it has been christened by the two other contenders, Romania and Canada, should see these two teams fighting it out for third and fourth positions and an early return home. After a good show by Canada in the 1991 World Cup, they have had a very disappointing build-up to the current World Cup campaign with heavy defeats by England, Scotland, France and New Zealand. They have also left behind their world class sec-ond row forward and captain, Norman Hadley, now playing for my club Wasps following a dispute with the coach earlier in the season. Unfortunately, they have not progressed since the

1991 competition but may well beat Romania. However, this will be a disappointing return for a country with high hopes of one day taking part in an expanded Five Nations Championship. Romania are likely to go home empty handed, also after a disappointing season which started with a 50-point defeat by England at Twickenham in November. France and Scotland should have no problem with Tonga and the Ivory Coast, although the Polynesian islanders can certainly be a hand full for any opposition with their more than aggressive defence. Some of the biggest hits of the competition are likely to come from Tonga or Western Samoa (in England's group!). The Ivory Coast are the surprise package of the 1995 World Cup, having defeated Zimbabwe and Namibia to qualify, an experience they are unlikely to forget, but one which unfortunately will not proceed beyond the pool matches.

In England's group, I believe we have possibly the toughest pool of all, with three contenders who on their day could cause us problems, namely Italy, Argentina and Western Samoa, all very different in their approach to the game. All three are capable of causing an upset. Recently Argentina have been in Australia on tour and despite losing both tests, the first by a heavy margin, in the second test they were leading Australia by 13-3 at half-time in Sydney, only to lose 33-13. They have an enormous pack of forwards and will certainly pose our own pack a number of problems, especially in the tight play, scrummaging and line-out. Their front row is one of the biggest in the World Cup and one of the best scrummaging units. They have a converted prop playing hooker, Frederico Mendez, now in his early 20s, who we first came across in 1990 at Twickenham when he was sent off for punching Paul Ackford with one of the best haymakers seen on the international rugby field for some time. He was then 18 years-old so he is certainly not frightened of playing with the big boys. The second row is also large and very competitive and will cause problems for Johnson and Bayfield. Behind the scrum they are less of a threat, although they have one or two exciting footballers, and will certainly miss the services of Santiago Messon, their full-back and main goalkicker who was injured in Australia, suffering a broken ankle.

This will be our first game in the competition and it is absolutely vital that we get off to a good start to take the pressure off for the rest of the group games. A defeat in the opening game would be catastrophic from an English point of view. As with any team, it puts you on the defensive right from the word go and we will need to put out our first choice XV for this game, especially upfront where we will be faced by a significant physical threat. The Italians are our second opponents and have improved greatly since the last World Cup when we also faced them as group opponents, defeating them reasonably comfortably at Twickenham. They have recently toured Australia, losing the series 2-0, but only by scores of 20-13 and 20-7, and more recently they defeated Ireland 22-12 in Italy as a final preparation for this World Cup. They are also quite capable of an upset and are very likely to be leading contenders, hopefully with England, from Pool B. They have a very capable pack of forwards, including the former Australian international Julien Gardner, now domiciled in Italy, and they have some experienced line-out men who played in the last World Cup. In the backs their key player will be Diego Dominguez, the former Argentinian international, also now living in Italy, who is an excellent goalkicker and playmaker of the highest order. Although defensively not very strong, he is one we will have to watch very carefully.

Our final group opponents on Sunday, June 5th will be Western Samoa, a highly competitive team who have caused some upsets in the last few years, despite losing some of their leading players to the New Zealand side, for example Steve Bachop and Frank Bunce who are this year in the All Blacks squad. Having beaten Wales on home territory last summer, they have had a couple of disappointing results recently, notably losing heavily to Australia and also in the last few weeks by 60 points to South Africa in Johannesburg. They are mostly famed for their defensive work and high, shoulder level spear tackling, which can be very dangerous, if not illegal. In the South African match, the Springboks lost four players through injury and this could clearly be a major problem for us only six days before we have to play a quarter-final knock-out match against either South Africa or Australia. Whoever is going to win this

World Cup will need a little bit of luck in the major knock-out matches and also with injuries, especially to key personnel.

So, who is going to win the 1995 William Webb-Ellis Trophy, currently held by Australia. Well, I think Pool A will be won by Australia, having defeated South Africa in the opening match in what is bound to be a very tense affair in Cape Town, not least for the way it will be refereed by Derek Bevan of Wales, who officiated in the 1991 World Cup final. He will set the scene for the way the rest of the referees will handle affairs. Refereeing is very important from both the technical and physical point of view. Certainly, South Africa will be very physical with a great deal of verbal intimidation. The way Bevan handles this will have a major impact on the outcome of the game. Also a couple of technical issues will be raised, namely lifting in the line-out, which the South Africans are very adept at doing, verging on illegality with regard to lifting before the man is in the air. The second rower can be supported once he is off the ground, but he is not allowed assistance to get him off the ground. This is not always the case in South African rugby. How the referees judge the playing of the ball on the ground will also be of vital importance to all sides and could well, along with the interpretation of the offside law, determine whether or not this World Cup produces exciting rugby or whether we are condemned to tense kicking affairs between both the tactical kickers and goalkickers. I see the Springboks as runners-up in this group with an early exit for Canada and Romania.

In Pool B, our own group, I expect England to win but have some difficulty in nominating the second string team. All three are capable of qualifying, although it will probably come down to Argentina or Italy. Maybe the Argentinian forward strength will prove vital in this area and put them in the runners-up spot.

In Pool C, New Zealand will win comfortably against Wales, Ireland and Japan, and the show-down is really for second place between Wales and Ireland. This is a very difficult one to predict, although the appointment of Alec Evans, the Australian taking over as coach of Wales, may just provide the impetus for them to overcome Ireland and therefore qualify for the quarter-finals. Another early exit for Japan and possibly for Ireland as well.

In the final group the main contenders are France and Scotland for qualification with Tonga and the Ivory Coast having very little chance of qualifying, although the Tongans, with their aggressive tackling, may again cause one or two problems. I expect the French to come out winners of this group and gain revenge for their surprise defeat in Paris in the '95 Five Nations. The winner will miss New Zealand in the quarter-final match and on this occasion I think France will have too much fire power for the Scots.

To the quarter-final line-up then, we could be faced with playing South Africa in Cape Town, being the number one game in the quarter-final draw. In the last World Cup we had to go to Paris to face France in the quarter-final and here again we could be lining up against the host nation on home soil in a knock-out competition. You could say this will be a big day! However, I am confident we have the fire power to overcome the South Africans, or the Australians, should they be our opponents. The other quarter-finalists could be Australia v Argentina, New Zealand v Scotland and France v Wales. The semi-finalists would then be New Zealand v England and France v Australia, a repeat of the 1987 semi-finals when France pipped Australia. This time I believe the roles will be reversed and Australia will venture forward to the 1995 final. In the other semi, England will just have enough legs and will power to overcome a very strong New Zealand to again meet Australia in a World Cup final. This time we are looking for a reverse of the 1991 result - and I do not believe I am dreaming!

The Final Gathering

Affter one final training session on Saturday morning, we at last gathered for the long-awaited departure. Since March 18th, the day of the Grand Slam decider against Scotland, this was the final meeting all the players had been waiting for. Weekly training at Marlow had continued the work started back in September, when, as a squad, we met following the previous South African tour and had decided that our goal for 1994-95 had to be to return to South Africa, "hit the ground running" in Durban, as Jack Rowell has often been quoted as saying, and start our campaign to try and bring back the Webb Ellis Trophy to England. Our preparations had gone as well as we could have hoped, having achieved a Grand Slam during the Five Nations and also beating Canada and Romania pre-Christmas.

Six out of six had been our target when we met in Bath in September for fitness training and now we were ready to leave. Despite meeting on the Tuesday, the flight out of Heathrow was not until Wednesday evening at 7.30 and we have yet more rounds of sponsors' lunches and dinners to attend and all the final kitting out necessary before any major rugby tour can begin.

The Petersham Hotel in Richmond has been the home of England rugby teams for as long as most people can remember. Certainly since my time with England, which started in 1985, the Petersham has always been our second home. There is a comforting feeling about driving up Nightingale Lane from the centre of Richmond to the hotel perched overlooking the River Thames and facing the great stands of Twickenham way up in the distance. Here we are meeting mid-morning on Tuesday, first of all to be kitted out in our

The press scrum at the Petersham Hotel before we departed for South Africa

commonly-known Number Ones, the England World Cup blazer, smart grey slacks, shoes provided by Church's, shirt and tie - all ready to look like an outfit meaning business. The England World Cup tie had been chosen by the combined input of the England backs at the session the previous weekend when the pre-designed tie was so awful the sartorially minded of our three-quarters decided that this would not do. John Elliott, the assistant manager, was despatched to Austin Reed to bring back a selection of ties more suitable. The final choice had been made on a show of hands, but the forwards were left to wonder about the choice of clothing the backs had let them in for. This was first evident at the sponsors' lunch on Tuesday, given by Scrumpy Jack, one of the three main England sponsors. Through our promotions company, Player Vision Limited, they were holding a small, select lunch at the Richmond Hill Hotel, 500 yards from the Petersham, for some of their customers. This lunch had been postponed from earlier in the Five Nations season when it is custom for the England team to entertain their sponsors at pre-match lunches. On this occasion we were entertained by our own Brian Moore and Eddie Butler, the BBC rugby correspondent and former Welsh international. Brian had drawn the short straw as being one of the senior members of the squad to give a short speech on behalf of the team. During the season, Will, myself and Rory have undertaken the dubious pleasure of speaking in front of our colleagues and now the final team lunch of the year belonged to Brian.

By the time we had kitted ourselves out in our Cellnet sponsored leisurewear, it was almost time to board the coach for another function, this time a dinner being given in honour of the England team by the National Sporting Club, sponsored by the Swiss Bank Corporation, at the Cafe Royal in Regent Street. Clearly, a lot of people put in a great deal of time and effort on behalf of the squad in fund raising and sponsorship, and also wishing to give the team the best possible send off for this hopefully historic tournament, although, inevitably for the players, sometimes these events can become rather tedious with a monotonous stream of repetitive questions about the competition. We know this is unavoidable but as you can imagine we just want to get on the plane, get out of town and get on with the playing. However, a very enjoyable evening was had by all at the Cafe Royal. We were entertained by a witty after-dinner speech by Jack Rowell, who somehow managed to lose track of time and spoke for 45 minutes. The players would have been delighted if he had sat down after ten minutes because most of the speech managed to contain anecdotes about the squad, which went down very well with the public. Victor Ubogu came in for some sustained leg-pulling from the manager due to his recent arrival in the superstar status with Jack keen to remind him he needed to concentrate on playing rugby again now that his well-publicised bar in Chelsea was open. Jack informed the gathering that Victor had come to him recently and asked why people had taken an instant dislike to him. Jack's rather sharp response had been: "Well Victor, it saves time, doesn't it." He also told the audience that Victor had turned up for training at the last session covered in love bites - all self-inflicted of course!

We were given a very enthusiastic send-off by the 600 guests attending this dinner and I think all the players left that evening knowing we were embarking on something rather special, that there was an enormous amount of people in the UK right behind us in the World Cup who were anticipating very strongly that we would return to these shores with the Webb Ellis Cup. I had begun to feel in the weeks leading up to our departure that the momentum was gaining and there really was enormous interest from the public. This was going to be the highlight of the summer for a great number of people.

Unfortunately, we still had another day to fill before boarding the South African Airways flight 353 to Durban via Johannesburg, leaving Heathrow at 7.30 on Wednesday evening. Wednesday morning was to be dedicated to official photographs outside the Petersham Hotel, but as always on these occasions the weather in the UK can never be organised as you want it and we awoke to pouring rain. The photographs were therefore taken in the small dining room in the hotel, first in our Number Ones (blazers et al) and then the Number Twos, chinos and smart shirts with a cotton jacket personally chosen by the Skipper for this trip. Apart from one or two of the trendies in the squad, this particular item of clothing met with some derision as we were fitting ourselves out for the photographs. Dean Richards presented a picture not quite resembling the sartorial elegance intended.

Despite being this great amateur game that we all play, most of the morning was taken up by various photograph shoots for our sponsors: leisurewear provided by Cellnet, sunglasses provided by Ray Ban - very necessary of course for the bright sunlight in Durban. How long will it be before rugby players walk onto the field wearing their Ray Ban sports sunglasses a la cricket players. Mark my words, it won't be long! Then there is the photoshoot for Laurent Perrier, official supplier of champagne for the England squad and their accompanying bright pink t-shirts. Let's hope we'll be needing plenty of their product as the tournament progresses.

At lunchtime we were finally through with the photographs and we then had a break until the official checking in time which was to take place in the hotel to save the hassle at Heathrow. I decided to slip off home at this stage, not living too far from Richmond, to say my last farewells to Sara and Beth. Our six-week old daughter. Emily, four and a half years old, is at school and I had bid her a fond farewell the morning before. It's always more diffi-cult for the girls on these occasions as rugby players are usually on tour for four or six weeks, possibly eight if it's a British Lions tour, which is obviously a long time, although not in terms of international cricket tours these days when players may be away for three or four months. Sara is used to such farewells as since 1986 I have been disappearing off to various parts of the world around May time, normally coinciding with her birthday, which does not go down too well. Here I was off again to take part in my third World Cup and leaving her behind with Emily and Beth. The only difference is that for the first time the wives and girlfriends of the England squad are being flown out at various stages during the World Cup to spend some time with us. In the past this has never been well considered by most of the players or administrators. This time, however, the players are grateful to the RFU for assisting with the cost of the trip for our partners. Sara was planning to come out with Emily and Beth, and her father Michael, to watch the Pool games in Durban against Argentina, Italy and Western Samoa. As far as Sara was concerned, this broke up the otherwise long trip and made the farewell less emotional than in the past. In ten days time we will be meeting again in Durban, hopefully after a relaxing 11 hours flight with the two young children and looking forward to a little bit of a break. Durban has the best climate this time of the year in South Africa and I hope this will give Sara the opportunity of having some relaxation as it is still warm enough to spend some time on the beach. Other wives and girlfriends are coming out at later times in the competition, either in Cape Town for the quarter-finals and semi-final stage - and then we are hoping they will all fly back to see us in the final!

On arriving back at the hotel everything is set for departure with our checking in sorted out and final calls to the office. I'm not sure if that's to make me feel good or to wind up my colleagues, knowing that I'm going away for four or five weeks. I have always been indebted to my employer, DTZ Debeham Thorpe, with whom I have been working since 1986, and particularly my close colleagues. In this instance, John Rigg, James Max, Jon Crossfield and John Page have to cover for me in my absence. English rugby players are generally well looked after by their employers and we are fortunate in this regard, more so than many other countries, a factor often overlooked by the RFU when considering the demands on the England squad. However, I have a very supportive company and they are interested in sport, rugby in particular, and I was given a very good send off by my colleagues who were genuinely hoping we would return successful. I must remember to ring John Page from the beach and golf course in our recreation time while on the tour. My colleagues appreciate me keeping in touch!

So finally the coach pulls out of the Petersham Hotel on the way to the airport. Not a good start for the duty boys of the day, Victor Ubogu and Steve Ojomoh, who allow the coach to pull out minus one of our team members, Graham Dawe, who was caught short at the hotel and was seen sprinting down Nightingale Lane to catch up with the coach. Our Press Liaison Officer, Colin Herridge, the former Harlequins' Secretary and a member of the RFU Committee, was heard to shout down the bus "You've left him behind" - "you" being the operative word. Colin, of course, was relinquishing himself of any responsibility and this was to come back and haunt him during the first day of the tour when he was awarded with our prestigeous 'Dick of the Day' award. Graham Dawe climbed aboard and we were off. At Heathrow we were ushered into the Business Class section of South African Airways, ready for departure.

On this particular flight we were joined by our Irish competitors, who were to be based in Johannesburg. The English and Irish have always had a good rapport, on and off the field, and we were delighted to be travelling with them. Many of us had toured together with the British Lions in 1993 and Nick Popplewell, the Irish loosehead prop, had this season joined my club Wasps, so we were looking forward to the Irish banter on the plane over. To begin with, though, we were separated in the Business Class lounges and the press were interested in the odd photocall of Nick and myself before departure. I had a chat with Brendan Mullin, with whom I had toured with the Lions in 1989 to Australia. Brendan is one of the most experienced Irish players and they had recently had an upset against Italy, who were in our Pool in Durban. He said the Irish had played very poorly that day in Treviso and that although the Italians were an improving side, he did not anticipate that if we were to play to our potential we would have too many problems with them. This was going to be Brendan's swan-song in international rugby, having already once come out of retirement, and he was looking forward to the World Cup, although he felt the quarter finals was the extent of the Irish ambition. He thought Irish rugby had a long way to go before being competitive in world terms and that really the Irish players and administrators had to get themselves serious about competing at this level.

Modern day international rugby players now travel Business Class, only introduced four or five years ago, following many years of travelling to New Zealand and Australia in Economy Class. Not that it's too much trouble for someone of my stature. But can you imagine Martin Bayfield and Wade Dooley cramped into Economy Class seats for a 30-hour haul to New Zealand and then getting off the plane to play international rugby only days later. It does not bear thinking

First Class all the way with the Skipper.

about. However, the administrators had now upgraded all international sides to travel Business Class and here we were on the plane with the Irish. Would there be enough seats? And if not, who would get the Business Class seats? My luck was in as I was given a boarding card for the First Class section of the plane. In one half of First Class was the English team, in the other the Irish team. Business Class had also been split up as well. More press photographs followed with the respective captains, Will and Terry Kingston, posing with a glass of the best South African champagne, sitting in First Class. It's a hard life!

I was sat next to Will for the flight over and it gave us an opportunity to dwell again on the events of the previous fortnight and our hopes and fears for the competition. We had spoken many times about our intense disappointment of the 1991 competition and how we had blown a huge chance to emulate our 1966 footballers who had won the big prize on our own soil. We both thought this would be our last World Cup and had only one thing in mind as we drifted off to sleep.

Thursday
May 18th

Sleeping Beauty! Victor enjoying the comforts of first class - much to the chagrin of Brian Moore.

After what seemed like a very short flight, with seven or eight hours sleep, I can certainly recommend First Class travel to anyone. As we touched down in Johannesburg there was some light-hearted mickey-taking from some of the boys who had been up in First Class, just checking if our Business Class team mates had survived the flight OK! Brian Moore was particularly upset, having been placed in Business Class when his fellow front row member, Victor Ubogu, had been given a seat in First Class with Steve Ojomoh. When asked by Steve why he had not been allocated a First Class seat when he had 55 caps, Brian's response, gruffly, was "59 actually", and no further comment was heard.

There was no great fanfare when we arrived in Johannesburg, or greeting for the team. We had to wait two hours before flying on to Durban and bade farewell to our Irish colleagues, wishing them all the best in the competition. After a couple of hours dozing and drinking coffee in the Business Lounge, we were on our way to Durban and the Holiday Inn, North Beach, where we would be staying for the next two and a half weeks before leaving, following our Pool games, hopefully to Johannesburg to compete in the quarter-finals.

The choice of hotel had been the subject of some debate earlier in the season when the England team management was informed that we must stay in the Holiday Inn Hotel, despite having requested the Rugby World Cup authorities that we be allowed to stay in an hotel of our choice just to the North of Durban. On our tour to South Africa the year before we stayed next door to the Holiday Inn and felt that it was too central and would be lacking in privacy when the hoards of supporters and local rugby fans arrived. We had, therefore, spent some time the previous year searching out a rather more secluded hotel, appropriately called the Beverly Hills, about 20 minutes North of Durban in a very exclusive resort known as Umlanga Rocks. Even though this would cost slightly more than the World Cup budget, the Rugby Union had agreed to pay the extra. However, the World Cup authorities insisted that we stayed at the Holiday Inn because they had booked all the teams into hotels of similar standard and felt it was only fair that all teams were on a level playing field. If this was the case, perhaps they should share all

the players around as well to make all the teams of an equal standard! The England management was particularly disappointed with this decision, but in the end had no choice. Not that
there was anything wrong with the Holiday Inn, but we had experiences in the last World Cup
which led us to believe it would be better preparation for the team to be away from the bright
lights of the city centre!

The rooming list had been sorted out and again I was to spend the next two and a half
weeks with my old school colleague and friend Rory Underwood. We have now been playing rugby together in the same team at fly-half and left wing for nearly 21 years, making our
debut in September 1974 at Barnard Castle School. We roomed together on many occasions
before on tours as far away as Australia and New Zealand. Rory is the official "duty boy organ-
iser" and it is his job to make sure the players given this title know what they have to do.
Primarily, their role is to make sure all the squad members know what is required of them
each day, the times of training, where and when meetings are to be held, and which social
events had to be attended. Failure to carry out these duties can be treated very seriously and
will normally be referred to "The Court".

One of the first duties on any major tour is
for the "Court Officials" to be put in place.
Damian Hopley, of Wasps, has assumed the
mantle of "The Judge" in the last 12 months
and on this occasion he will be supported
by "The Chief Prosecutor", Brian Moore,
alias The Pitbull, who has held this position
since his entry into the squad in 1987. He in
turn is assisted by "The Court Enforcers",
Dean Richards and Martin Bayfield. The
"Clerk of The Court", is Dewi Morris, and
the "Finesmaster", yours truly who has
been included as a court official for the first
time in his career. The "Defence Counsel"
will be provided by Kyran Bracken, who
unfortunately in these cases has a particularly hopeless task. It is also customary to
appoint an anonymous "Chief Sneak" to
report any offences to "The Judge" or any
other "Court Official" so that the papers

My roomy and former school pal Rory Underwood.

can be prepared for the next session. He is known as the infamous "Mr X" who appears in
disguise at all the court sessions. It may appear to be a good thing to be one of the court officials during the course of the tour when punishment is dished out on your team mates.
However, this has a habit of backfiring at the "People's Court" at the end of the tour when
the official court officers are overturned by the rest of the team and rather severe punishment
is meted out to those who had previously been dispensing such punishment.

Having settled in with my roomy for the next two and a half weeks, we ventured out with
other members of the squad after a bite of lunch to browse along the seafront and reaquaint
ourselves with what is a very pleasant place to spend this time of year. Only 200 yards down
the beach is the favourite haunt of last year's tourists, Joe Kool's, and hopefully this year it will
be less frequented by the squad with more serious intentions ahead. Clearly, though, the odd
light refreshment would be required during the course of the next fortnight and no doubt Joe
Kool's will be one of the more well attended of the possible venues.

Already it is clear that the humidity and heat are going to cause some concern and the
medics are busy making sure we understand the importance of taking on plenty of liquid in
our daily diet, as well as trying to keep out of the sun as much as possible. Factor 15 will be

at the ready for our daytime training sessions. Training for the first evening is planned at 5pm at one of the training pitches adjoining Kings Park, the home of Natal Rugby Union, and a test venue for South Africa which will host all England's Pool games, plus a quarter-final and a semi-final. The starting time of 5pm is chosen because this is the kick-off time for the Argentina and Italy games with our other Pool match being at 8pm against Western Samoa. Judging by the humidity on our first afternoon in Durban, we are delighted that 5 o'clock kick-offs have been deemed appropriate. Kicking off at one or two o'clock in the afternoon would not have been to our liking, despite the benefits gained from humidity suits worn in training back in the UK.

We were couped up for 48 hours prior to departure, with little physical activity, and as is normal the first session is meant to be a light stretch, supervised by physio Kevin Murphy, a stalwart of the England team. He had quite deservedly won the "Unsung Hero" award at the RFU's annual dinner on the Thursday prior to departure at which Martin Bayfield was nominated the England Player of the Year. This awards dinner was notable for the huge cheers from the 600 members of the audience at the London Hilton every time Will Carling appeared on the giant screen showing action from the previous season. Dennis Easby was there to present the Player of the Year award and was shuffling uneasily in his seat, wincing at each showing of Will. To avoid any further embarrassment, Will was not present at the dinner due to a previous engagement. I'm sure that was the case! Kevin Murphy has been with the England team as long as I can remember and is one of the most respected physios in British rugby, having also been on the last two Lions' tours of 1989 and 1993. His daily routine of warming up and stretching exercises are filled with much humour and despite the regularity and ultimate monotony of such routines, he is very popular with the troops.

Following Kevin's normal procedures, Jack decided it would be a good idea to have a few gentle run throughs with 15 against 11. The squad is made up of 26 players, normally 14 forwards and 12 backs, which does not allow you the luxury of two full teams for practice sessions, as normally the case on an overseas tour. It does provide sufficient members, however, for sensible opposition. I could sense the boys were raring to get stuck in although Kevin would have been happier had we restricted this opening session to stretching and limbering up exercises rather than run the risk of muscle tears following the long trip. However, Jack let us loose on each other and although he implored us to stay at 50 per cent effort, clearly the term "half pace" does not enter the vocabulary of this particular squad. Within a few minutes the session was turning into a serious level of contact as World Cup action had finally begun.

The mood of the camp was spot on and I think it had come as a relief for everyone that we were in our place of destination to start training for our opening game against Argentina. The atmosphere was very different to 12 months earlier when, although on a serious rugby tour of South Africa, itself a great challenge, the mood was on a different level with no need to psyche up the squad. It was more a case of holding people back until the right time. The Argentina game seemed light years away and the way we were training we would be lucky to reach next Saturday without several losses to injury inflicted on each other. It already seemed an eternity since we left the UK, but now base camp had been set up and the England World Cup 1995 assault had been launched at Kings Park in Durban, Kwazulu Natal.

Friday, May 19th

The routine was now set for the next week with training days falling into a pattern of breakfast between 8 and 9 am, meeting at 9.30, leave for morning training at 10, back for lunch, possibly a double session of training at five in the evening, change for dinner, probably a team meeting before dinner and if there was any energy or time left, perhaps we might pop down the road for a beer or a Coke to fill in the final hour of the day and back to bed. A very monotonous routine and one which needs to be broken up with either changes in training or social events and recreational activities such as golfing, fishing, cinema, possibly even shooting with our security guys.

Day two in Durban was to be our first big double training session of the campaign. The big danger for me is that we are over a week from our opening game against Argentina and a normal Five Nations build-up would only involve four training sessions, the previous Sunday morning, Wednesday afternoon and Thursday and Friday mornings before going into one of the major matches of our domestic season. Now we are faced with over a week with two sessions on certain days and my fear is that by the end of next week either the edge will have gone from training or the players will be so much on edge their performances will be affected by the long build-up. Only time will tell. From past experience of the last World Cup, and also the Five Nations preparations, I am anticipating the tension building among the management as well as the players.

Our second day in Durban starts with breakfast in the team room on the second floor of the hotel, an area not accessible to the public where we can keep ourselves to ourselves before training. You will find most modern rugby players are now accustomed to a breakfast of cereal and fruit, followed by toast and tea or coffee. The days of large fry-ups have all but disappeared. It's not easy to go into a full-blooded training session with a stomach full of bacon, eggs, mushrooms, tomatoes and perhaps the odd bit of black pudding, although there's not much of that to be found out here.

The first offenders appear on the "Finesmaster's" sheet with "The Judge" handing our lateness punishments to Backy and Hunts. Team discipline, both on and off the field, is very important in such a competition and we have always prided ourselves on our excellent self-control on the field, even under serious provocation. This discipline often begins off the field where time keeping for meetings and training is very important. "The Judge" will not be lenient on such misdemeanours. Fines are normally used at the end of the tour to subsidise any shopping required, or more often than not, spent in the bar.

Jack explains what we will be doing for the first serious day's training in World Cup '95, and we board the coach for King's Park again. The massed ranks of the media are in abundance and from now on we will have to get used to TV cameras being poked under our noses from South African Television, Sky, BBC and ITV, along with the journos, not to mention the snappers from the UK daily newspapers and the freelance boys with whom we have a good relationship and who assist with promoting our sponsorship deals. Onto the coach and the ritual of numbering off, which may be unique to rugby. Just before departure the tour numbers are called out by each individual to establish if anyone is late. Any missed calls incur the wrath of "The Judge" and the "Finesmaster" is kept busy.

The back seat of the coach on the way to training and matches is historically the domain of the forwards, going back three or four years with the likes of Winterbottom, Teague, Dooley and Brian Moore, a bit like our days at school when the seniors occupied the back seats, and nobody dare encroach on this sacred area. However, there appears to have been a slight shift of power over the past few years and now the back seats are occupied by the likes of the Skipper, myself, Rory and Dewi, while Brian Moore is the only stalwart from the forwards stamping out his territory. As backs we will have to wait and see how long we will get away with this incursion into forward land. I don't think our bravery will last long!.

Friday morning sees a sweltering day in Durban and between 10.30 and 12.30 the boys are suffering a little in the heat. Coaches always say training will be short and sharp and last an hour and a half max, but inevitably it is two and a half hours before we finish. Again, however, the intensity and commitment from the players is 100 per cent. The gathered crowd, I feel sure, are impressed by the organisation and effort put into training by this England squad.

Training has become somewhat of a military exercise in terms of organisation, often run by Les Cusworth, with a lot of ball handling skills for the whole squad, something which we have been keen to work on in the last 12 months to improve everybody's ability in this department, particularly those of the forwards who have improved significantly. There's also contact work on the tackle bags and pads with a great deal of emphasis on ball retention. Again we are generally very good at winning first phase possession but need to maintain this possession when taking the ball into contact and recycle possession five or six times if necessary before creating scoring opportunities for our flyers on the outside. Then there is the ritual split of forwards and backs, with the forwards doing more heavy contact work and scrummaging, and the backs going off to practice their strike moves and handling skills once more, particularly concen-

The forwards give it their all in the sweltering Durban heat.

trating on lines of running and depth in attack. This is something that English backs are poor at and an area where there is great concern among the senior players and Les. We finish by coming back together again for some teamwork to get the forwards and backs working together. This is an area where Will is concerned we do not spend enough time and he would like to see Jack concentrating more on this rather than splitting backs and forwards, which has always been the way training has been carried out in English rugby. We feel it is necessary to move away from this to a degree to integrate backs and forwards playing together to improve our overall game. By mid-day it is sweltering and we are looking forward to returning to the hotel for a short rest after lunch to give the legs a break before the five o'clock training session. These early days are always rather intense from the training point of view, with the management trying to pack in as much heavy work as possible so that later in the week the legs can be rested in the hope that by Saturday there's enough energy and enthusiasm left to take on a major international.

Back at the hotel food is always a major issue for rugby players and the Holiday Inn have opened up their restaurant specifically for the use of the England team, both for lunch and dinner. The hotel is quiet at the moment, although we are expecting a great deal of supporters arriving at the end of next week when our privacy will be undermined. It is only then the players will realise why the management were keen to have us in a hotel 20 minutes out of Durban. For the moment, though, things are pretty relaxed and we are not hassled too much. As for the food, once again our dietary needs have been considered by Rex Hazeldene, our fitness advisor from Loughborough University, who arrives tomorrow and has instructed the hotel to provide us with soup and sandwiches at lunchtime. Some of the forwards muttered under their breath that this was not sufficient and they were looking forward to Rex arriving so they could tell him exactly what they feel about the dietician's view on life. After a spot of lunch, a quick shower and an hour's relaxation in our room, it's time to get ready for training session number two.

Following my visit to South Africa last year with England and also the Prime Minister's touring party in September, Sara had bought me the autobiography of Nelson Mandela, a 600-page tome which I am determined to finish by the end of this tour. I am not one of life's great readers at home, apart from the newspapers, and I will be very pleased with myself if I can manage to finish the great man's book. I hope in four and a half weeks time I will know even more about his great struggle and "Long Walk To Freedom", as the book is titled.

Five o'clock comes and we are off again, this time under lights at King's Park. The enthusiasm of the squad remains strong. Mike Catt and I stay behind after the session to do some punting and goalkicking together, work which is very important but often overlooked in team sessions. Therefore, it becomes the responsibility of the individual required to carry out these tasks after training has finished. Our kicking guru, Dave Alred, who I have worked with in the last 18 months, is arriving tomorrow with Rex Hazeldene, and one or two other members of the England entourage, and no doubt he will be keen to catch up, having missed out on the last couple of days.

Back at the hotel, fed and watered, Jack wants a chat with some of the senior players and his closest management to discuss various social and tactical issues. So following dinner, Will, myself, Brian and Deano are summoned to Jack's suite on the 30th floor - obviously he needs a big room to plan our assault on the World Cup and to entertain visiting dignatories, and we are delighted to be invited to the inner sanctum. John Elliott, the assistant manager, and Les are also present. Many issues were discussed and clearly there is an enormous amount of experience, with the four players having been involved in nearly 200 internationals between us, and also Brian, Deano and myself having played in the two previous World Cups.

Selection is obviously a key issue, particularly as we play three games in a week before going into the knock-out stage. It is not the same as a tour when you have two teams and generally find yourselves splitting into one team playing on the Saturday for the major games with the second string playing on the Wednesday, thereby providing a weekly match for each player. Here there is consideration of resting players in that first week without disrupting the team too much for we cannot afford to lose any of our games. Coming first in our Pool is clearly the aim of the first part of the competition. Therefore, one needs to balance the desire to play your best team all the time with the need to make sure that at the end of the first week we have not suffered too many injuries and the leading players, especially the forwards, are sufficiently rested. In an ideal world we would like all the forwards to play two games each. It is less of a problem for the backs, but with only one front line fly-half in the squad and Mike Catt, normally a full-back, as the back-up, there is a discussion about whether I will play three games in the first week.

We also talk about the possibility of substitutions for injuries, however spurious, towards the end of games if this is deemed a sensible thing to do, without disrupting the team too much, to allow a player to rest for the final 20 minutes. Individual areas of selection are also discussed in some detail, particularly the form of one or two players and their mental state coming into such a difficult and challenging competition. The mental attitude of players, as well as their physical condition, is especially important in the knock-out stages where your World Cup future depends on the next 80 minutes. John Elliott was keen to pencil in the three sides for the Pool games so that we had some idea who was going to play and how many matches they would be getting. In the end we had a general discussion regarding how we would try and restrict the number of games, particularly for the forwards, but it was felt

The Pitbull soaks up the sun in Durban...

impossible to pencil in the players due to injuries that may take place, always likely in a World Cup.

Already Dean Richards was carrying a slight hamstring strain which we were all intrigued to know how he picked up as speed has never been one of Dean's strengths. Maybe it had something to do with the long flight. All the players were keen to ensure that training in the first week was varied and not too lengthy to keep interest high and a freshness in the build-up to the first game. Once we were over the Argentina match, the competition would move along very quickly, not only because we would be playing ourselves, but because of the many other games taking place which would form a focus of interest for the squad. We are all looking forward to the opening game next Thursday between South Africa and Australia.

...Jason Leonard and Dewi Morris doing likewise.

Saturday, May 20th

S omebody in their wisdom - or lack of it - decided on this particular day that all 16 teams would meet in Cape Town for an official opening lunch ceremony at the Groot Constantania Wine Estate, between Cape Town and Stallenbosch, for the Rugby World Cup Directors to officially welcome all participating nations. There had been something similar in the 1991 tournament held in London on the day that all the nations assembled, and then the feedback from the players was that there was really no need for this, indeed there was no interest whatsoever from the playing fraternity. However, once again the administrators had decided they would like all the teams to be in Cape Town, but we are still unsure who benefits from this gathering. It certainly wasn't the players; we had to spend ten hours travelling for a two-hour lunch at which we did not want to be present and which appeared to serve no purpose, other than for the administrators - or "Blazers" as they were commonly known at the lunch - to have a jolly good time.

We left the hotel at 7.15 am to be driven to the airport where we sat in the departure lounge with the Argentinian team, also based in Durban - the England squad at one end of the room, the Argentinians at the other. Our plane finally arrived half an hour late from Bloemfontein, in the centre of the country, where it left with the Welsh and Japanese teams on board. The unfortunate Welsh had been up at five o'clock to catch a plane that had to fly due east to Durban, pick us up and fly all the way back across South Africa to Cape Town on the western coast. You can imagine that even by 8.30am when we got on the plane, the Welsh were not best pleased.They also had to face the long trip back from Cape Town to Durban to let us off the plane and then fly on to Bloemfontein later that evening, a totally ridiculous situation.

On arrival in Cape Town we were greeted by a cheering band of black and white minstrels and several groups of schoolchildren who were obviously delighted to see the teams, along with a typical early winter rainstorm which continued for most of the day and as normal shrouded Table Mountain in low cloud.

As the team boarded the coach to be led in convoy by police outriders to the lunch, I was collected by Edward Griffiths, the new Chief Executive of the South African Rugby Football Union (SARFU), to be whisked briskly off to Newlands, the headquarters of both Western Province Rugby Union and SARFU, for a brief handing over ceremony of the first batch of kit collected in the UK for the South African Rugby Union Development Office for distribution in the townships. This initiative was prompted by my visit in September 1994 with Prime Minister John Major and his delegation, which included myself, Sir Bobby Charlton, Sir Colin Cowdrey, Alex Stewart and heptathlete Judy Simpson. We spent three days travelling around townships in Cape Town and Johannesburg seeing what assistance we could give. The UK Sports Council announced during this trip that they were setting up a sports initiative, backed by the Prime Minister, in the hope that private and public funds could be invested in black South African sport. The two sports considered to be in most need were soccer and athletics. Cricket is also very keenly played by the blacks and in September we visited the new cricket pitch provided in the township of Alexandria with British money where an England A match was played the previous summer.

I had returned to England moved by the plight of the young sports people in the townships and the chronic lack of facilities, including basic items of clothing for the children in which to play the sport they clearly loved. Several weeks later I appeared on the Rugby Special programme and on the spur on the moment, with John Inverdale's assistance, requested publicly that if anybody was considering throwing away their rugby kit, could they send it to Wasps Football Club where I would see that it was transferred to South Africa. Little did I know the response I would receive and the headache I would give my club administrators at Wasps having to deal with all the kit which for the next six months came flooding in. However, with the

help of dedicated colleagues at Wasps, and John Scott, the head of International Affairs at the UK Sports Council, we were able to gather in excess of two tons of equipment to be forwarded to South Africa with the valued assistance of DHL. By the end of April, they had collected all the kit from Wasps and were ready to ship it out to South Africa. The first consignment had already been received by Sas Bailey, the head of the SARFU Development Office who I had met the previous September. We had hoped to gain some

Will Carling receives his World Cup cap from Sir Ewart Bell - was this the reason for our ten-hour journey?

publicity for this initiative while in South Africa and decided my brief visit to Cape Town would provide the best, if not only, opportunity for the press to get some pictures of the official handover.

Edward Griffiths had only just taken on the post of Chief Executive of SARFU and had been given the difficult job of controlling politics in South African rugby. Unfortunately, as in most sports all over the world, the leading administrators engage much of their time in fighting politics within the organisation and wasting useful time that could be put to assisting the sport in their own country. Edward had been in the job six weeks and was already finding that several members of the South African Rugby Union Committee were not talking to him. It sounded to me very much like the RFU Committee and the England squad.

In our brief chat in the car on our way to Newlands he highlighted yet again the difference between rugby administrators in the Northern and Southern Hemispheres. The previous morning in Cape Town a meeting had been held between the heads of the respective South African, New Zealand and Australian Rugby Unions to discuss ways in which they could further assist their players to gain more financial reward from rugby union and had agreed to set up a joint company to look into opportunities. They are very worried about the threat from rugby league and are not prepared to allow this to diminish their pool of top international players. They discussed ways in which they could raise more money through selling TV rights for all Southern

Hemisphere provincial and international matches and thereby create promotions companies which would have more money to be distributed to the players. This they expected to be in place by the beginning of the next domestic season in the Southern Hemisphere and they were confident they would not lose too many of their leading players. In fact, the South Africans were openly persuading their players not to sign on rugby league terms before the negotiations currently being undertaken were finalised. The publicity surrounding these negotiations can only help to improve the position of the Northern Hemisphere players with their unions, so we were not unhappy to see these talks taking place.

We have, in fact, been talking to the Rugby Union for the past three or four months to set up a joint sponsorship deal with a major company whose name would appear on the England shirt for the first time ever, with the spoils being shared between the players' company and the Rugby Union, a total package in the region of £1.5 million per annum over the next four years leading up to the 1999 World Cup. This is currently being negotiated while we are in South Africa and we hope to announce the formal signing of such an agreement in the weeks following our return to the UK. This will be a major breakthrough in Rugby Union/player relationships and we are aware that following the retirement of Dudley Wood at the AGM in early July, there are many members of the Rugby Union Committee who feel that this provides an opportunity and a watershed for relationships to improve. Certainly, there is some improving to be done, but I do believe that everybody in the new order would like to see things get better. All this pressure from the Southern Hemisphere is assisting our cause. To be fair to the Rugby Union, a great deal of work has been done in the last few months by Richard Field, the Union's Marketing Director, and Malcolm Phillips, a former England and Lions' centre, who is the committee man with responsibility for the new Players-Union Working Party. He has worked hard behind the scenes with his fellow committee members to proceed matters. Our view is that this is a once-every-four-year opportunity to work together as the players certainly have enough irons in the fire under their current arrangements up until the next World Cup. I believe a golden opportunity will be missed, certainly in PR terms for the Rugby Union, if this is not taken up. The next few weeks should prove very interesting.

Once the photographs with Sas Bailey and a few press interviews were completed at Newlands, Edward and I raced off to catch up with the England team. What should have been a very picturesque setting on a beautiful day turned out to be a wet and miserable occasion for the marquee lunch set in the grounds of the Wine Estate. True organisation seemed to be lacking and by the time the organisers got around to saying grace most of the teams had demolished the starter and were already looking forward to the main course and getting back onto their planes.

It is true to say that most international rugby teams generally have a very good relationship, both on and off the field, save the odd personal battle which is inevitable. But the last thing teams want to do prior to a big game is to mix socially and consider the niceties of the World Cup competition. We are here to do a job and the players just want to get on with the training and playing. For the majority of the lunch most of the sides kept themselves to themselves, but we were very conscious of being eyeballed by the Western Samoans who were clearly looking forward to our encounter on June 4th, our last Pool game.

I spoke to several players from most of the leading nations and came to the conclusion that not one of them wanted to be here on this Saturday afternoon. Jason Little and Tim Horan, the Aussie centres, were seen in heated conversation with Jeremy Guscott and Will Carling, albeit friendly banter, possibly the four best centres in world rugby who have a very good relationship off the field. Tim Horan was back in the Australian squad after dislocating a kneecap only 12 months earlier, a very serious injury suffered ironically in Durban in the final of the Super Ten series between Queensland and Natal. He was still not back to partnering Jason Little in the Aussie midfield and had not been picked for the Australian side to play South Africa next Thursday, but would no doubt be looking forward to challenging Daniel Herbert who had taken his place.

I also had a brief chat with Christian Califano, the French tighthead prop who had been one of my playing colleagues in Toulouse. He was then just starting off on his senior club rugby career and now, three years later, found himself in the French World Cup squad. He had already played against us at Twickenham earlier in the season. This coincided with the extra-ordinary sight of seeing the whole of the French back division with shaven heads. Up in their training camp in Pretoria the French had clearly already become bored with their existence and in what no doubt appeared to be a very entertaining idea at the time was now not quite so funny. It's certainly the sort of thing one might expect from a group of French forwards, or indeed any forwards for that matter, but to see the likes of Franck Mesnel and Phillippe Sella with shaven heads was not a pretty sight. Sella was not best pleased with his team mates who had obviously put him up to this. On reflection I couldn't help thinking it was not really the sort of thing Jeremy Guscott, Will Carling, Rob Andrew and Rory Underwood would do. However, it did create a light-hearted discussion point over the lunch while the 16 captains were invited forward by Sir Ewart Bell, the Chairman of Rugby World Cup, to collect their 1995 World Cup caps and the individual ones for each member of their squads. This appeared to be one of the few reasons we had been invited to the lunch; perhaps next time they could find some way of delivering them to our hotel, or at least have the lunch at a single point of arrival for all teams on the first day of the competition, rather than allow teams two days to settle into their training routine and then drag them half way round South Africa. Who said it was a game for the players?

Victor Ubogu seemed to spend more time with the Ivory Coast team than with his English colleagues and was clearly aiming to run for President of this small African state once the World Cup was over. I am sure "The Judge" would have noticed his behaviour! If not, there were plenty of people around to inform him.

On finally leaving the lunch, Will and I were able to catch a quick word with Bob Dwyer and Bob Templeton, the Aussie coach and assistant coach. They were looking forward to their encounter with South Africa and deep down I think Will and I were quite keen they should win this game so we did not have to meet Australia in the quarter-finals. Not that we did not think we could beat Australia, but we were both hoping for a repeat of the 1991 final when we could take our revenge. We wished them all the best against South Africa and looked forward to meeting them at Ellis Park on June 24th. A small gathering of rain-sodden supporters wished us well on our way

Will and Jerry pictured with Aussie centre Tim Horan at the opening gathering in Cape Town

from the lunch and we were delighted to be heading back to the sunnier climes of Durban.

The other more serious aspect of this lunch was that Deano had managed to claim a slight hamstring problem the day before in training and had therefore been excused the lunch by Jack so that he could stay behind for treatment from Kevin Murphy, or "Smurf" as he is known. There were serious accusations on the plane on the way back that this had been a cunning plan conceived by the pair of them to avoid a boring and tedious Saturday. Again I fear "The Judge" will take retribution.

Sunday, May 21st

T he previous day seemed just a bad dream as we awoke again to blue skies, looking down on a crystal clear blue Indian Ocean from the 17th floor of the Holiday Inn.

One thing about a day off, even though it was enforced and unnecessary, is that it does keep the boys fresh and sharp for training. Our mid-morning session in the heat was lively and some of the contact sessions in the team work were becoming rather fierce. Often in such sessions there is little regard for the safety of yourself or your colleagues as the battle to prove your commitment in front of the selectors is clear for all to see. This can often boil over to flare-ups between individuals, even club team mates back home, and this morning Martin Johnson and Graham Rowntree, of Leicester, decided that over robust play on both sides of the divide warranted the swinging of a couple of haymakers and a few sharp words.

I have rarely seen this happen on international duty back home but I have witnessed it in World Cup preparations where there is a battle for places with the knowledge that some individuals may not get a game in the whole of the five-week competition. That happened in 1987 with Jeff Probyn not playing and also in 1991 with Dewi Morris and David Pears being the only two players in the England party of 26 without a game, even though we went all the way. Nobody wants to be in that position during the World Cup and points are there to be proved. In 1991 we had some very strong training sessions with tempers boiling over on several occasions between what otherwise were regarded as the best of buddies off the field. Johnson and Rowntree play in the same club side week in, week out and by mid-afternoon they were on the best of terms again.

By now the England touring party entourage was complete with the arrival yesterday of Dave Alred, the kicking expert, Rex Hazeldene, our fitness expert, and Dr Austin Swain, our sports psychologist, also from Loughborough University, who had been spending time with us during the domestic season, assisting players who thought they could benefit from his advice. This has not been forced on anybody and I have to say that rugby players as a group are generally fairly sceptical about the needs of a sports psychologist. Often they feel they have coped well enough in the past to get them to the top of international rugby and that they can blooming well cope in the future. However, we are constantly finding that having reached the summit of international sport anything that can give a team the edge at the margins may well prove to be the difference between ultimate success and failure. There is very little to chose between the top sides in world rugby, or for that matter the top sides in any international sport, and if an edge can be achieved in any area, this has got to be considered. Fitness training and dietary considerations are becoming fairly standard across the world, and positive thought and improved technical excellence are what is required next. We still have a long way to go in these areas compared to American football or basketball where the psychology of sport plays a big part. We have made giant strides on the technical side and the inclusion of Dave Alred in the England squad is an important part of this. Having spent 10 years playing international rugby, to only have had proper coaching in kicking from a technical viewpoint in the last 18 months indicates how far behind we have been in the use of such expertise.

Dave has spent the last six months working with myself and Mike Catt on an individual basis and he was hoping during this World Cup to find time to work with all our backs, particularly on the punting aspect which has become more important for all players to carry out efficiently. One only has to look at the prolific punting distance of David Campese as a winger to prove how important this is. One 60-yard kick in a close, tense quarter-final or semi-final, as opposed to a 20-yard slice into touch just outside your own 22, which gives your opposition the throw, may be the difference between winning or losing the World Cup. Dave is hoping to spend the whole of the competition with us and from a personal point of view I am pleased about this, having worked successfully with him, particularly on the goalkicking. No-one needs to tell me how important this may be in a World Cup. Once we get into the competition, when the team training will be less heavy, he will have more time to spend on individual coaching with the scrum-half, centres and wingers.

Today has been decreed a one-training day which allowed us the luxury of a relaxing lunchtime barbecue on a private beach, just to the north of Durban. This is one of the more acceptable and sociable parts of a rugby tour and the boys revelled in the surf and sand. As part of our World Cup sponsorship, Cellnet have generously provided us with mobile phones for our exclusive use. Several of the yuppie members of the squad can now be seen wandering around the hotel and on the beach with phone in hand, and even the captain has been caught on film on the training field with his mobile. Several could be spotted walking up and down the beach ringing the UK just to keep family and friends informed that everything was OK, despite the toughness of the training regime. Damian Hopley was ringing his brother and fellow Wasp Phil just to let him know that life was not too tough here in Durban and he hoped his elder brother was not worrying about him too much. I did think about calling Sara on this lovely Sunday morning, but on reflection felt I was better advised to leave such a call until later in the day when life was perhaps not as enjoyable as here on the Indian Ocean.

Rex Hazeldene had advised us earlier in the morning that in this humidity it was important to take on lots of liquid and to rehydrate as often as possible, including taking our daily ration of salt tablets. Alcohol was not on the list of liquids to be consumed and in fact was positively discouraged. Jack had decided that there was no need for any childish curfews or alcohol bans completely, but common sense had to prevail. Our doctor, Terry Crystal, however, as well as being very good at Bill McClaren imper-

It's a tough life on tour - relaxing with the boys on a private Durban beach.

sonations, was keen on the odd drop of alcohol and, on seeing the boys drinking can after can of Diet Coke, felt he could not let the side down. The only thing is he was spotted by one of the sharp-eyed sneaks refilling his Coke can from a bottle of best South African white wine. I fear the prosecution is already building up a large dossier for the first "Court" which is yet to be called.

Monday, May 22nd

Countdown has begun and Saturday, May 27th is within sight. Jack has decreed that we will have a double training session today as he feels there are still lots of areas where we need to tighten up before our first game. The team is to be announced this morning so the XV can start concentrating from the afternoon session onwards.

Before leaving for training we have the standard 9.30 meeting at which Don Rutherford, the Technical Director of the RFU, has prepared dossiers on our three opponents in the Pool games. Before concentrating on the Argentinians later in the week, we are to look first at the Western Samoans. As with all teams they have different patterns of play which they become accustomed to, depending on the nature and size of their players. The Samoans are very mobile and aggressive and caused many problems in the last World Cup, narrowly losing 9-3 to Australia in their Pool and then beating Wales to take the Pool runners-up position and thereby consigning Wales to pre-qualifying for this year's competition.

The focus of the video was on how the Samoans like to keep the game fluid and play a little bit like the Fijians, a 15-a-side version of sevens. If they are allowed good possession and are able to run with the ball, they are a very dangerous side. They are also equally as dangerous when you have the ball as their tackling is probably some of the most ferocious which will be seen in the World Cup. Certainly this particularly video, showing clips of their victory over Wales in the summer of 1994, demonstrated how dangerous their tackling can be. We also studied their recent defeats against Australia and South Africa, who both adopted similar tactics to disrupt the Samoans, namely using their heavy forwards to win possession and drive at the Samoans, keeping the ball fairly close and not allowing them the opportunity to run free. All this was put away in the memory bank to be used later in the competition.

Will has constantly instilled into the players the need for more personal responsibility before and during training to discuss with the coaches and management what we feel is required. When there are players with the international reputation of the current England squad, it makes sense to draw upon and use this experience when organising training. A lot of players can have an input, but it is still down to the management to decide exactly what we are about to do. Often the tensions which are building up in the playing squad are also having an effect on the management and sometimes this is taken out on the players through the lengthy nature of training sessions, often going over old ground and only serving to build up the tensions within the squad.

The side was announced at lunchtime and on returning to the hotel, following another kicking session with Dave Alred, I discovered that my old partner Dewi Morris was back in the England side to play Argentina on Saturday. Dewi had played in both tests in South Africa last summer and also in the opening test in England against Romania, but had since been replaced by Kyran Bracken, who played against Canada and throughout the Five Nations championship. There is very little to choose between the two players and this was the only major change from our victorious Five Nations side. Dean Richards' hamstring has proved not to be the spoof we all thought it might be on Saturday as a ploy to watch the FA Cup Final between Everton and Manchester United, but appears to be more serious and he has been kept out of the side as a precaution. A long-term casualty at this stage would not be in our interests. Steve Ojomoh will take his place at No 8, having performed extremely well on all occasions he has been called upon by England in the last 18 months. Otherwise the side has a familiar ring to it with Jack obviously deciding the importance of a win in the opening game outweighs any thoughts of resting players and keeping them fresh for the later stages.

So this is our first World Cup '95 XV: The backs are as per the Five Nations with Mike Catt at full-back, the two Underwoods on the wing, Carling and Guscott in the centre, myself and Dewi at half-back. The front row is the well-known combination of Jason Leonard, Brian Moore, Victor Ubogu, backed up by Martin Johnson and Martin Bayfield, with Ojomoh joining Ben Clarke and Tim Rodber in a very explosive and mobile back row. This is a big chance for Dewi to stamp his authority back onto the England side and one I know he will be very keen to take, having given up his job five months ago to concentrate on the preparations for the World Cup before starting a new job on his return to the UK. He has worked very hard on his game in the last three or four months and I think this knowledge, plus the fact that Kyran has not played a competitive game since the Grand Slam decider against Scotland on March 18th, probably counted in favour of Dewi over Kyran.

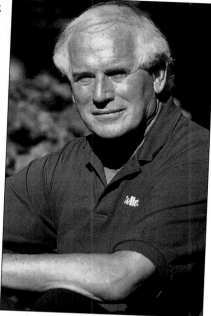

The manager Jack Rowell - putting us in tight corners to see if we can handle the pressure!

I spent part of the afternoon on the phone back to the office in London, a habit on tour, to keep in touch just in case they decide to fill my desk with someone else. As always there are one or two things that are outstanding following a departure for such a length of time. I always find it is best to call the office from the hotel late afternoon when I can inform them I have just finished training, or about to start another training session. Much better to do this than ring from the golf course in the middle of the morning. Somehow that is not well received!

The evening session was a shambles. We were out at five o'clock to acclimatise and sometimes we have these sessions where the whole thing is very disorganised and Jack appears to be challenging individuals and putting them in tight corners to see how they can handle the pressure. I noticed this through one or two of our Five Nations matches and always felt he was seeking to ask questions of the players. Some of them find this difficult to respond to and get more and more frustrated as the session goes on. This to my mind was exactly one of those sessions. We had discussed the previous evening how we felt training was going and one of the words that came up was "frantic", meaning a lot of effort was going in and people were keen to impress but we needed to just calm things down and be a bit more focussed on what we were trying to achieve. We finished the session with some rather heated discussions and one or two very unhappy senior players who were reaching boiling point. I am sure Jack does this on purpose to keep everybody on their toes, to make sure the players go away from a session not thinking they are God's gift to rugby but, quite the opposite, that there are a lot of things to discuss and get right. And just when you are about to explode Jack announces, quite unexpectedly, that there will be no training tomorrow. Everybody is to switch off, go away and enjoy themselves and we will reconvene for training on Wednesday.

Tuesday, May 23rd

I have been on many major rugby tours, beginning in 1987 with the first World Cup and including two British Lions tours in 1989 to Australia and 1993 to New Zealand, both lengthy eight-week affairs. Few coaches are prepared to give the boys a day off from training. Maybe the occasional Sunday after a Test Match well into a long tour, but to be given a whole day off only four or five days into the World Cup preparation is almost unheard of.

Not that there is anything wrong with having a day off, far from it. But most coaches and managers feel obliged to work the players, in some cases only to justify their existence because they feel if the players are not flat out they are not doing their job properly. In fact, a day off can be the best remedy for all sorts of ills, both physical and mental. I have heard it said that on cricket and football tours the management drive the players so hard they have to beg the coaches to take it easy on them. This certainly happened in the 1977 Lions' tour to New Zealand and also, I understand, in the 1990 soccer World Cup in Italy. A balance has to be drawn between training and recreation and it takes a wise man to see this.

Maybe this training lark gives us a taste of what professional rugby would be like. Training every day with few other interests is something I am not particularly interested in. So Jack has done his usual trick of winding everyone up to fever pitch and then just at the point when everyone has had enough, he sends us away to cool off and forget about rugby.

So what do you do on a day off in a strange place? Obviously the squad's interests are very varied and while some are happy to laze around the pool reading or listening to music, others like to get out and be a bit more energetic, maybe on the golf course or deep sea fishing. This is what Dean Richards wanted to do yesterday morning, but three hours deep sea fishing at six o'clock in the morning followed by training had not gone down too well with the management. During the last World Cup several members of our party had taken an interest in clay pigeon shooting. This will be difficult to arrange in South Africa, but the security boys had certainly set up a shooting gallery with their colleagues in Durban. The police officers in our squad, Martin Bayfield and Dean Richards, were keen to test the firearms used by the South African Police. I thought it best to keep away from this particular activity, bearing in mind what happened in the last World Cup when John Olver forgot he had taken the safety catch off his shotgun and very nearly blew Peter Winterbottom's foot off. Boys will be boys!

The more sedate members of the squad were up early for an 8.30 tee-off at the Royal Durban Golf Club. Usually we find that golf clubs are very accommodating on tour and are delighted to receive a small group of players, hopefully those who can at least hit the ball, even if it is not always in the right direction. The sight of Jason Leonard, Brian Moore and Victor Ubogu charging down the first fairway is not a sight that most golf club secretaries appreciate. Certainly those on the other fairways are in grave danger from the flight of uncontrolled golf balls.

A 7.30 call summoned Rory and I to an early breakfast before meeting in reception where several of the players were joined by Les Cusworth and Dennis Easby, President of the RFU. One or two of the boys had remembered to pack their golf shoes, but not many had the gaul

Golfing on our first day off.

to bring their own clubs. The sight of the England squad at Heathrow with kit bag under one arm and golf clubs over the other shoulder would not have given the right impression. However, coach Les Cusworth, an ardent golf addict, somehow managed to sneak his clubs onto the plane without the boys knowing and suddenly they appeared ready for action. "The Judge" would have to be informed.

Before we departed some skulduggery had gone on with regard to the drawing of partners for the nine holes we were about to play. Jon Callard and Phil de Glanville informed the Skipper that he had been drawn to partner Dennis Easby in a two-ball. Surprisingly, this did not go down terribly well with Will! Using captain's prerogative, he insisted that a redraw take place with him being present. So Will had managed to escape spending two hours with the man who two weeks ago had sacked and reinstated him as captain.

The first four-ball was away with Dennis Easby partnering Les Cusworth, playing against Austin Swain, otherwise known as "Spook", and Jon Callard, whose skulduggery had backfired in the redraw, being partnered with the management. Second away was the three-baller, Carling, de Glanville and Underwood T., and the final three-ball was brought up by myself, Rory and our chief security man, Steve, who informed us that this was only his fifth game of golf ever - and Rory and I felt we could be in the money here!

Steve had been with us last year when there was a significant amount of security required as our tour coincided with the first democratic elections in South Africa. We had arrived in Durban just after there had been several disturbances in the Kwa-Zululand area of the country. In fact, only two weeks earlier New South Wales had refused to travel to Natal to play a Super Ten game because they feared for their safety. Fortunately, by the time we arrived everything had calmed down and we saw no evidence of any trouble on our visit last year. This time round all of the countries were very closely guarded by some of the top policemen in the South African force who are normally on diplomatic duty looking after the top politicians in the country, including the President, Nelson Mandela. For South Africa, this opportunity was too great for there to be any slip-ups. They were under the watchful eye of the rest of the world for the next five weeks as they staged the first major world sporting event in South African history. The word had come down from above that no chances were to be taken with any of the teams. Our security boys felt this was a complete overkill, but clearly it would be a total disaster if anything did go wrong. On our arrival there had already been some bad press in the UK newspapers about the level of violence in Durban, and although much of this we believed to be irresponsible journalism, there were dangers involved with certain no-go areas. Often these situations are made out to be much worse than they are. Had there been any danger at all, the players would not be allowing their wives, girlfriends and young children to come out to Durban to watch our World Cup games. As in any major city in the world, there are areas where you would not venture after dark, but I felt very confident about bringing my family out here to spend the week watching the Pool games.

Walking round the Royal Durban Golf Course was very relaxing after five days of hard training, although I have to say the quality of the golf was not too much to behold. One or two of the press had compared Dave Alred and his kicking coaching to David Leadbetter's golf coaching with Nick Faldo. My golf is certainly in need of something - but it may need more than

David Leadbetter to sort out my swing. Rory and I had played on many golf courses on previous rugby tours, and although too much golf can be a little tiring in the week of an international, the odd nine holes is a pleasant way of switching off. Neither of us play to a particularly high standard as we have had little opportunity to spend a great deal of time on the golf course, but we both enjoy a good hit every now and again. Some of the boys, including Jeremy Guscott and Jon Callard, played yesterday at the Durban Country Club where much of the course overlooks the beach.

The Royal Durban Golf Club is situated within the Royal Durban Turf Club, where we have been invited on Sunday to spend an afternoon in the Stewards' Enclosure for one of the many horse race meetings in Durban. This is not the most picturesque course in the world but very enjoyable all the same, although the rough is rather difficult to get out of - and I should know. Coming up the 18th fairway I was tempted to call my colleague John Page in the office, a very keen golfer and a member of Moor Park Golf Club, just up the road from where I live. We have promised we will get a game in one Sunday morning. Unfortunately, this has not happened and I fear there may be a sense of humour failure if I was to call at 10.15 on a Tuesday morning.

Approaching the final green, my approach shot was not the most accurate, but I was lucky that the clubhouse overlooks the 18th. As my rather overhit eight iron shot rebounded off the clubhouse onto the green, I think Dennis, the club manager, was beginning to wonder whether it was a good idea to let this group of English rookie golfers onto his course. Nine holes was enough for Rory, Steve and I, and Will had also given up on his group who were continuing for 18 holes. We adjourned to the verandah of the clubhouse to get stuck into bacon and egg sandwiches and black coffee with the hot African sun beating down on three very lucky Englishmen.

While we were waiting for the remainder of our party to finish their 18 holes, Will and I decided it was time we had our hair sorted out before the first game on Saturday, and Dennis recommended a hairdresser not far from the golf club. Haircuts are always a topic of great humour among the squad, regardless of the quality of the coiffure, and Will and I knew we would be in for some ribbing. Fortunately, she was not the one who had been employed by the French backs and we were both relieved to come away reasonably presentable. Not that it made the slightest bit of difference to the comments when we got back to the hotel.

We returned for a light lunch and a couple of hours lounging by the pool on the 32nd floor of the Holiday Inn, which overlooks the whole length of the golden Durban sands. The police marksmen were just departing for their afternoon's activity and we hoped we would not lose any of them before tonight's meeting. Our very own South African beach bum, Mike Catt, formerly from Port Elizabeth, now of Bath and England fame, decided he would entertain us with his body boarding. While we watched from our vantage point high above the beach, the ITV cameras rolled for even more material for their programmes back home. The ITV guys, Jim Rosenthal, and cameraman Ian O'Donaghue, had spent most of 1991 tour with the squad and had built up a very good rapport with the team.

After a relaxing afternoon, Dave Alred suggested it might be a good idea to have another kicking session. One of the set-backs about being the goalkicker is that a great deal of extra work has to be done to make sure this most individual of skills is carried out to a high standard. It can be quite lonely at times, putting in the additional training this requires, particularly back home on evening sessions when everybody else has shot off to the shower and bar while you are still out doing your training in the wind and rain of England's deep winter.

Kicking out here in South Africa is not quite so arduous, even in the evenings, and we decided to do a session under lights. The sun is just about going down in Durban at five o'clock and so off we went with our security guys who follow us everywhere. Apart from ensuring our safety, they are useful for retrieving balls, especially those which are caught in the trees behind the posts on training pitch number one at King's Park. Their own kicking and retrieving has improved considerably in the short time we have been here and their help is much appreciated. Dave is a bit of a workaholic when it comes to kicking technique and practice and we go through a whole routine of exercises and drills which incorporate not just goal-kicking but punting, up and unders and kick-offs, all of which in their own way are just as important as goalkicking. The full-back and fly-half have to do the majority of kicking in any rugby team, but Dave has been keen to work on the rest of the backs. Now, at the end of each training session, we have a ten or 15 minute drill, with a series of kicking exercises for all the backs, and testing every other day for the punting to see if players can keep the ball within a ten-yard channel kicking down the field. It's amazing the effect a little bit of competition has on training and the message is finally getting

Rory and I with Jim Rosenthal and cameraman Ian O'Donaghue outside King's Park stadium in Durban

through to all backs that extra kicking practice is needed. Dave is finding that the afternoons are filled with several players engaging in coaching clinics with him.

We start with a gentle warming up exercise, punting the ball in the five-yard channel between the touchline and five-yard line, which normally marks the start of the line-out. This is also designed to test the kicking lines of the player, the whole focus of Dave's technique being to make sure the ball travels in a straight line with all of the power from the leg going up and through the ball, rather than the foot making contact with the ball and then hooking or slicing, which often occurs. A bit like my golf really! Any slight deviation off the foot is shown up when you are working in only a five-yard channel, and although not much power is being put into this exercise, it is a good discipline to keep the shoulder, head and leg in line, having made contact with the ball. We then move into the ten-yard channel, between the five-yard and 15-yard lines, which gives you the impression of loads of space after working in the five-yard channel, and we also start to put a bit more leg into this exercise. Anything outside this channel is deemed a failure and we will work in this area for 15 or 20 minutes, effectively playing tennis with a rugby ball. A little bit like hitting a golf ball straight down the centre of the fairway, there is a sense of achievement in striking a rugby ball cleanly off the foot with it spiralling away from you, nose down, in a dead straight line. If only it was as easy to execute as it is to talk about.

Having spent some time on this drill, we usually finish by having a lane assessment with the player taking five kicks from each end of the channel, these being graded as to distance and direction so that a measure of consistency can be taken at each training session. Suddenly the player is placed into a pressurised environment. Having been happily kicking the ball backwards and forwards with his partner, he suddenly has only himself to battle against in a ten-yard channel which is narrowing by the second. It is difficult to replicate the pressures of a game in training, but for punting this is one way to do so and more often than not the technique goes to pieces, with the ball ending up anywhere but in the channel. This is where a good physical technique, and also a mental focus, becomes important so the battle is not against the need to keep the ball in the channel, but purely a technical battle which, if the exercise is carried out properly, you know from experience will result in five out of five landing on target.

The same can be said of goalkicking where in the heat of the moment you have to have the confidence that your technique, both mental and physical, will hold up, even if it is in the 79th minute of a highly charged international when this kick may decide the game. All too often this is the case and only the very best goalkickers are able to cope with this pressure. I will never forget being on the receiving end of a Grant Fox 43-yard penalty in the last minute of the first Lions' Test in 1993. We were leading 16-15 when New Zealand were awarded a penalty to win the match. It was almost inevitable that Grant Fox would send the ball sailing high between the posts to win the game - and he did.

Again for our goalkicking practice, it is not just a question of taking hundreds of shots at goal from different positions and angles, although clearly this does form part of the process. Of more importance is grooving a technique so that the follow through stays straight, having made contact with the ball, and the head and shoulders stay down on the ball until long after it has gone over the posts. So often people are looking to see if the ball has gone over, almost before they have taken the kick. With the head and shoulders opening, it is very difficult to keep a straight follow through. Keep your head down and believe, almost through an eye in the top of your head, where the ball is going and picture it. You don't need to see where the ball has gone; everybody else can tell you that. Because of this, we spend a lot of time kicking along the try line towards the posts, aiming to hit the near post. This is the best test of all to see how straight you are kicking the ball. There is no margin for error with this exercise and we spend a lot of time trying to drive a line from the ball to the top of the near post.

Having mastered this, we have several different exercises which we carry out. One involves taking kicks from the 22 bang in front of the posts where we are only satisfied with getting the ball down the middle of the middle, right at the top of the uprights. Anything slightly to the left or right would be acceptable to most people, in that the ball has gone over, but from a technical point of view it means we have not quite struck the ball cleanly in a straight line. We also do a circuit of 33 kicks from specified areas of the pitch, both in front of the posts and from different angles, right and left, and a more difficult exercise, taking 24 kicks from the right-hand five metre line, starting just outside the 22 and moving in towards the try line so by the end of the exercise you are kicking from three and six metres from the try line. Again this tests any hook on the ball as from that angle it is impossible to get the ball through the posts unless you have a straight line follow through and the trajectory of the ball is in a straight line.

By the time we have finished with a few drop-outs and I have put up a few timed high balls for Mike to catch, nearly two hours have passed and we are both mentally and physically exhausted. For the high ball practice we like to have a measure of the hang time of the ball in the air and its relationship with distance. A hang time of just over four seconds for a distance of between 30 and 35 metres is about ideal for the supporting chasers to arrive just as the ball is coming down. They can either compete for the ball in the air or hit the catcher the moment he takes the ball and try to turn him on our side so we can regain possession.

One thing for certain is that the kickers will not be short of practice on this trip and there are several sayings that keep us going for the many hours of lonely training. Dave likes to use "Whatever it takes, practice makes perfect" as a commonly recited expression. I like Gary Player's saying in his prime when he used to come out with "The more I practice the luckier I get", which is a good answer to those who like to say, when somebody has done well, that "the luck was with you today".

I am a great believer that we knock our top sportsmen too much in the Northern

Dave Alred puts Mike Catt through his paces in yet another kicking practice session.

Hemisphere. Sometimes I even get the feeling that aiming for excellence on the sports field is frowned upon. That is certainly not the case in the Southern Hemisphere where excellence is highly praised. Practicing to be successful is a common trait which runs through South Africans, New Zealanders and Australians on the rugby front. It is about time we started to encourage excellence on the sporting field and competition within our younger people. I firmly believe that competition is a good thing. In every other walk of life you do not get rewarded for mediocrity.

By the time we had returned to the hotel, showered and had a dinner with the team, Mike and I were feeling that our one day off so far had not exactly been a holiday, but we both agreed that the more work and practice we can bank now the better it will serve us later in the tournament. Before collapsing to sleep after a few more pages of "A Long Walk To Freedom", I made a quick call to Sara to find that she had awoken with a stiff neck the morning before and was in the middle of physio treatment at home and not in the best of spirits. Unfortunately, two young children, particularly Beth at six weeks old, do not take into account that Mummy is struggling to move and things seem a bit fraught on the end of the telephone. But Sara is looking forward to coming out on Saturday morning to see the first game.

Coach Les Cusworth - in his time one of the most inventive fly-halves in English rugby.

Wednesday, May 24th

B eing stuck in the middle of a major competition, it is often difficult to appreciate the interest that surrounds us back in the UK. We are also making a special effort not to read too many of the local newspapers as they are full of different theories every day as they try to fill their columns with so-called considered thought. Often, it's not very considered at all. There are an enormous number of journalists covering the England team for the national newspapers back home and relationships are generally good with the rugby press, although we had been informed that the tabloid newshounds would be arriving shortly, just in case there was any scandal they could drag up about us or any of the other sides taking part. This is obviously the unacceptable side of international sport, but I'm afraid it's a fact of life which leading sports people have to deal with. We have always been very fortunate with the responsible way which our game has been covered by our rugby correspondents and long may this continue.

On this particularly morning, after breakfast in our usual meeting room, news had broken that the England players were about to sign a new sponsorship deal in conjunction with the RFU for a figure approaching £1.5 million per annum for the next four years leading up to the 1999 World Cup. During the last three or four months a small committee consisting of myself, Brian Moore, Tim Rodber and Mike Catt had been set up to look into commercial opportunities which existed on a joint venture basis between the Union and the players. This was the first time we felt significant progress was being made with the Union as in the past the outgoing Secretary Dudley Wood had always maintained it was not the Union's job to make money for the players. This entrenched view had got the Secretary and some of the leading members of the Union into difficulties with the players and was one of the main reasons why the relationship was so poor between the administrators and ourselves. The way forward was for a joint action between players and Union whereby both could benefit and broken fences could be mended. Malcolm Phillips was keen for this to happen and negotiations were underway with five or six leading companies to sponsor the England team and have their logo on the actual England match kit. Our's would be one of the last of the Unions to agree to this, having seen Australia, New Zealand and South Africa do so many years earlier.

Many of the British journalists had been taken aback by Peter Jackson's article in the *Daily Mail* which speculated that the deal was already in place and the players would be receiving half a million pounds towards their kitty from next season, while the Rugby Union would be taking £1 million out of the sponsorship for their funds. Ian Robertson, the BBC Radio correspondent, decided he would run the story as an exclusive, saying the deal was about to be signed and this would be an historic step in the history of rugby. We were besieged with questions on the coach to training about what this meant for the English players. Unfortunately, no one was in a position to comment because, although several of us were aware of the delicate nature of the negotiations, nothing as yet had been signed and it was unlikely that anything would be for several weeks, certainly not until our return to the UK. Even then it was not certain there would be a satisfactory conclusion to the negotiations and this was a classic case of the media looking for a story, having been out here for several days. There is only so much you can write about when the action has yet to start.

Having had a day off from training, the boys were keen to get back into things as we were now on the final countdown to Argentina. We are able to focus totally on the Argentinian threat and begin our standard Five Nations build-up from the Wednesday to the Saturday. The warm-up was again taken by Kevin Murphy, with ball skills conducted by Les Cusworth. The improvement in our ball handling over the last 12 months has been significant and I always think we look a better side in good conditions. We are starting now to get the game play and team work operating smoothly. After the warm-up we once again split into backs and forwards, the backs concentrating on lines of running and depth. We are a self critical team which spends a lot of time analysing videos of both training and matches to see where we can make improvements.

The backs have been critical in a constructive way of each other and feel that although we want to lie reasonably flat to get across the gain line quickly, we also need to hold a bit of depth, especially out wide with the full-back and wingers to give them more time when the pressure is on from highly aggressive defences. There is no doubt that this will be the case in this World Cup. We also work hard at keeping our lines of running straight and parallel to the touchlines to ensure we hold space for the outside runners and not have the whole back line drifting across the field, which makes life much easier for defenders who can pick players off as they run towards the touchline. We set up a camera in the stand of the main stadium to catch us on video in our training sessions, which gave a good end-on view of our lines of running, to be analysed later this evening.

The other area which is very important, particularly in this World Cup, is the ability of backs to carry out forwards' duties when the back row is not able to get in support of the back line. "Backs supporting backs" is one of Jack's great issues. In the modern game backs have to carry out rucking and mauling techniques like any forward. The thought in days gone by of backs doing this would not be well received, but the modern game is so fast and physical that often the back row is not able to get into support. The backs have to recycle the ball themselves, which may mean the forwards coming on as second wave runners and having to have the handling skills of a three-quarter. As with many major sports, the basic changes in the last ten years have been significant and many players of past eras would find it difficult to cope with the pace and power of the modern game. Not that the modern game is any more entertaining or interesting - it is just a fact of life.

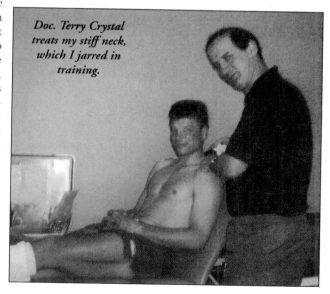

Doc. Terry Crystal treats my stiff neck, which I jarred in training.

After staying on to do a brief kicking drill, I returned to the hotel and made my first visit to the medical room on the 17th floor to receive some of the magic workings of physio Kevin Murphy, having woken that morning with a stiff neck which I jarred when doing tackling practice at the beginning of training. Maybe I was coming out in sympathy with Sara, but whatever the reason a good massage and manipulation from "Smurf" was definitely required.

Somehow Kevin has been able to put players back on the field within days of injuries which looked completely debilitating. I remember, on arriving as a replacement for the 1989 Lions' tour, following the unfortunate injury to Paul Dean, the Irish fly-half, in my enthusiasm to impress I had done some extra sprint training only to find that my hamstrings were still on the plane and within seconds I felt the infamous twinge in my right leg. Keeping this to myself, I quietly conferred with "Smurf" who looked as me with one of his frowns and got to work with the ice and flowtron. I had been selected to make my debut for the Lions against Queensland Country three days later and went onto the field with my right leg heavily bandaged and not knowing whether I was going to make it. Only Kevin's ability on the physio's couch and the confidence he gave to me, as he does to so many other players, allowed me to go 100 per cent into the game, having been told that I would be fine. As always he was right!

The backs were summoned to a 6.30pm video session with Les and Will to consider what we had done in training that morning. One of the difficulties with any form of training is trying to replicate match situations in a false environment on the training field. We felt the exercises we had done this morning were carried out reasonably well, although we were still not happy that they were a true representation of what would happen in the game. Old faults were still present, however, and often with many of the issues at hand it really is down to a state of mind. When players are concentrating on what is required, we are able to carry things out to a high level. The problems occur when players have more than one or two things to think about at the same time and then there is often a breakdown in the execution of an earlier skill we had been concentrating on.

It is not easy to overcome these problems, but we are now experienced enough that we can sit down, analyse videos and be critical of each other without people throwing their Teddy Bears away and the whole thing becoming a personal slagging match. This would not have been the case several years ago, but there is now a maturity among the backs and a understanding of each other's moods that most people know how far they can push an issue before it becomes counter-productive. To say we are a moody lot would be an understatement, and as Les Cusworth often points out, he needs the "Spook" to talk to him about the behaviour of the individuals in our back line more than he needs him for his own sake. As always, more hard work and concentration were deemed to be the solutions to our problems and no doubt there will be plenty more of this in the coming weeks.

In the evening we had been invited out to the Sports Cafe in Durban, one of a celebrated chain across South Africa run by a Canadian company, very much a North American idea. One has recently opened in the Haymarket in London. The idea is that everybody goes with their friends, drinks a few beers, has something to eat and sits glued to television screens showing sport from around the world, either on video or by live satellite. It's great for sports lovers but not very good for conversation. At this particular one in Durban, which I have to admit we visited on the odd occasion on our trip to South Africa last year, there are something like 140 television screens plastered around. We had been invited as their guests to have dinner that evening, which always sounds a good idea, but in reality you feel a little bit like an animal in the zoo, caged up eating your food. Many of our England supporters are here and we are grateful for their support, although at times it can become a little bit claustrophobic, both in the hotel and out socially, trying to get away from talking the niceties of the game. Just for good measure, the Sports Cafe had very kindly arranged to show a re-run of the South African-England second test in Cape Town last year when we went down to a pretty heavy 27-9 defeat - South Africa's first home victory since their re-emergence into world rugby. A little bit like the Australians, the South Africans have a habit of rubbing things in when they are on top, but are not too keen when the boot is on the other foot. However, that having been said, we were rescued by live coverage of the Ajax-AC Milan European champions final which we found much more palatable along with a good meal. Unfortunately, the self-imposed alcohol ban prevented us from hanging around too late.

Thursday, May 25th

D-Day for World Cup 1995: the opening ceremony from Cape Town followed by possibly one of the matches of the competition, the hosts South Africa against the holders Australia in Pool A, the day all South Africans and rugby lovers across the world have been waiting for.

We are not training until after the first game, and therefore have the morning free before sitting down to watch the opener. To relax and fill in time, I thought it would be a good idea to hit the Royal Durban Golf Club once more for a further taste of their hospitality. This time there were not so many takers for the 9.15 tee-off, as several of our party are keen on their sleep and were much happier lying in bed rather than chasing a golf ball around. So it was down to Jon Callard, Phil de Glanville and myself to see if we could improve our handicap. Hard though it may be to believe, I was even worse than I had been on Tuesday, and decided again after nine holes this is not really my sport and that I must get some proper lessons. I decided to quit gracefully while I still had a couple of balls left in my bag.

We went back to the hotel for a leisurely lunch and a relaxing early afternoon to watch what I had predicted to be a reasonably comfortable Australian victory in the opening game. The television crews were interested in seeing our reaction to the first five minutes of the game and Colin Herridge allowed them to hang around the team room filming us watching the Aussies and South Africans set forth.

I had not seen the opening ceremony of the 1991 World Cup as England had been involved in the first match against New Zealand at Twickenham. While we were deep in the bowels of the old West Stand, the celebrations were going on above us. This time I made the effort to sit and watch the opening ceremony in Cape Town and was struck by the excitement surrounding the whole day, both within the crowd and in the South Africa Television commentary box. It was almost as if people could not contain themselves. This was no doubt one of the biggest days in South African rugby, if not sporting history.

What then followed was probably beyond the wildest dreams of most South Africans. Either they were playing a very canny game, or they played far above the expectations of most of the South Africans I had spoken to in the week we had been in Durban. Even at the Golf Club this morning we could not find anyone willing to take a bet on a South African victory. Most people hoped they would put up a good performance and only lose by a narrow margin. What happened could easily have graced the World Cup final with a magnificent performance by the whole of the South African team, who, quite honestly, made the Australians look ordinary, no mean achievement. Apart from an early penalty goal from Michael Lynagh to put the Australians in the lead, it became apparent early on that the South Africans were in the mood for this match and it was clearly going to be difficult for the Australians to match them. Whether the Springboks were up for this game to a level they had not reached before, or whether it was the fact the Aussies were slightly below par which allowed the South Africans in, was not easy to identify. Often in these cases, there is a small element of both which contributes to the outcome. As it was, although the Aussies won a reasonable amount of line-out ball through John Eales, some of which was not particularly high quality possession, generally the South Africans were sharper and quicker around the field and more aggressive in the tackle and chasing of kicks. In simple language, they looked as if they wanted it more. At the highest level of international rugby, where there is often little technical difference between the two sides, this simple statement can often be the deciding factor. If one could only bottle the ingredients which produce such an all-round team performance, you would be a very rich man. We in the England squad have often talked about how on some big occasions we can raise our game to previously unattainable levels, yet at other times with the same players turn in a performance not worthy of those taking the field. I have been involved in several of these ups and downs in international rugby and we are still searching for a solution.

The South Africans this afternoon were unremitting in their desire for victory, and I don't think I have seen an Australian side make so many mistakes or look so uncharacteristically ordinary in their play. David Campese had a shocker, which, bearing in mind his popularity in the England squad, went down well in our team room! Maybe on the evidence of this performance, it will be just as well if we do not have to meet South Africa in the quarter-finals in Cape Town. A repeat of this performance, or indeed their performance against us in Cape Town 12 months earlier, will leave us very stretched. But will they be able to hold on to this form? On the other hand, will the Australians play as badly again in the competition? Assuming we now win our group and they come second in their's, it will be Australia we will be meeting in Cape Town in the quarter-finals and not South Africa. It seems we cannot escape - but let's win our Pool first!

This was the signal that the competition was at last underway and we were in the final countdown to our opening game. We were now down to the last major training session before our Saturday match, as the Friday is often a cosmetic run-through, more through habit than necessity, with no real emphasis placed on the physical nature of the training. However, the Thursday is a very important session and for this we were allowed access for the first time onto the main King's Park pitch at five o'clock. Following the end of the Australian-South Africa match we boarded our team coach and headed for the stadium. Even in our hotel there was already an atmosphere of euphoria among the South Africans, and on arriving at King's Park we were faced with a large crowd which had gathered at the stadium to watch the international in several of the private boxes that are a feature of South African rugby grounds. Clearly the party had started and we were greeted with a volley of generally good natured banter regarding the quality of the South African performance. It was almost as if South Africa had already won the World Cup and their countrymen were in a mood for celebration. We reminded them, of course, very politely, that the final was not until June 24th and a good performance today, although significant, did not mean they had won the competition. However, this victory had set them on their way, and with the winner of Pool A going into the easier half of the knock-out draw, with the toughest competition coming from France, this obviously gave South Africa a better than even chance of making it to the final.

Will surprisingly announced that evening there would be no Friday training session, which is often handed over to the captain by the manager. We had discussed this in the past as a squad and Will and some of the backs felt quite comfortable with having no training session on a Friday before a big game, preferring to use the time to rest our legs. The forwards, however, preferred a light run-out and doing a few line-out practices to get into the groove and spend time together. It's more of a habit than being of any great practical use at this stage in the preparation for a major game, although habit and environment for players at such a pressurised time is often important. The Skipper felt we had done enough work, having been together the better part of ten days in the build-up to this game.

This evening's team meeting was reasonably relaxed in the circumstances and we were confident we knew what to expect from the Argentinians, having studied their videos closely. A favourite theme of Jack's is to have no surprises from the opposition that might catch us out. From watching the videos, Argentina are obviously going to present us with a physical challenge, but a none too sophisticated game plan.

Friday, May 26th

The day before a big game is always the worst in my experience in that time tends to drag and players get very nervous thinking about the possible outcome of a match which is not to be played for another 30 hours. This is when we would have a normal training session which would fill in a bit of time for the players. For the last 18 months I have always had the luxury of keeping myself busy with extra kicking practice, if one can call it a luxury. Often at home players occupy their Friday afternoon by calling the office, reading or wandering around the shops before the evening meal and then, perhaps, a trip to the cinema. Some find it difficult to sleep and may even request the doctor to hand out the sleeping pills to get a good night's rest.

With no team training today, Dave and I decide to do an extra sharpening up session before our planned five o'clock kicking practice at the stadium under lights. We are both sticklers for making things as perfect as possible and obviously there is a danger of overdoing things on the practice field, although we both felt things had been a little rushed yesterday and using time sensibly today would be no bad thing.

With our trusty ball boys from the South African Police Force, we wandered around the corner to the Argentinian training ground mid-morning to do an hour's session, mainly of contact work on the ball and driving a line through the ball with a much shorter run-up of only two paces. This was a specific drill to concentrate on contact and line rather than putting the whole thing together and we were happy with our efforts. Between then and five o'clock, when we would be going back to the stadium, it was time for relaxation on our rooftrop hideaway, although Will had declared that all those playing in the game tomorrow should keep out of the sun before kick-off, a wise precaution in the Durban heat.

The rooftop, however, proved to be a perfect vantage point for prying into the Argentinian training session, which started at 11.30 and went on for a full two hours in the hottest part of the day. As far as they were concerned, there was no need to rest. Either they felt they had more work to do, or they needed to sharpen up. In any event, it was a long and tough session the day before a major game and not one we ourselves would be accustomed to doing. Much of their practice was based around the scrum - no surprise there - and also some pretty heavy defensive work against tackling bags and shields, clearly aimed at disrupting our midfield and back-row runners, which we hoped to launch at them to create holes in second and third phase possession.

After concluding our spying mission on the Argentinians, I spent the rest of the afternoon on the phone to my office in London and also speaking to a client in Hong Kong who I had been trying to get hold of for most of the week, via France and Italy, now finally catching him in the Far East. I was in the final throws of trying to complete some business when Dave and JC called to say it was time to go off for the next training session. And to think in the office they believe I'm on holiday!

In between times I had managed to catch a glimpse of the opening Scotland game against the Ivory Coast. In half an hour Gavin Hastings has scored 29 points, which obviously puts my world record of 30 points in jeopardy. By the end, the Scotland and British Lions' captain had amassed a massive 44 points in one single international against the hapless Ivory Coast, a record, dare I say, which will last for some considerable time. Scotland were over their first hurdle without too much trouble.

The competition was now in full swing and later in the day Tonga were to give France a scare, particularly in the first half when they should have been leading had they had a goalkicker of international standard able to finish off one or two clear cut chances. In the end they lost their shape and discipline and Steve Lander, the English referee, became the first man in the middle in the 1995 World Cup to send off a player for illegal use of the feet. France took advantage to run in four tries in the second half to finish comfortable victors, not really a satisfactory start for them, though. And finally in the evening, Canada and Romania met as the second game in the group of death, with Canada running out comfortable 30-point victors against a poor Romanian side, now destined to meet Australia and South Africa before returning empty handed to Eastern Europe.

The stadium lights were on full beam as JC, Catty and myself arrived with our kicking guru for one more session. This time we were under less time pressure, although the Argentinian kickers were following us onto the ground a little later. We decided, after some punting practice to warm up, that we should do a cir-

More kicking practice in the Durban twilight

cuit of 33 kicks in our standard format. For some reason I was not feeling too good at the start of this session. In fact, I was being put under pressure by Catty, who was striking the ball really well, outkicking me in the first 20 attempts at goal. JC, on these occasions, likes to do his own routine which he has fashioned for himself in the last couple of successful seasons at Bath. Our ball boys were scurrying to all parts of the seating behind the posts with three kickers peppering them.

I was beginning to get a little bit frustrated by my kicking and was perhaps starting to look for excuses. I told Dave that I thought we had done too much in the last two days and I had slightly lost the edge to my kicking. The whole thing had become routine. I am generally not a stabber or chipper of the ball. I need to be in an aggressive mood to strike cleanly up and through, bringing a great deal of effort and concentration into each kick. Dave could see through my excuses and forced me to work hard for the last 13 kicks, to battle back through concentration, and by the end I had finished with 12 out of the final 13 successful kicks at goal. Although mentally I was very tired by the exercise, Dave felt we had earned some money this evening, his way of saying it's all in the bank and will be vital when the pressure is really on for the game itself.

I managed to get back to the hotel in time to give Sara a quick ring before our team meeting at seven o'clock. I caught her before she was leaving for Heathrow with Emily, Beth and her father Michael, ready for their adventure to Durban. I was very much looking forward to seeing them tomorrow after the game.

Jack was tense at the team meeting, which was mirrored by the players. I was not sure whether this was cause or effect, but either way it was a rather stuttered meeting and one which went over old ground we had covered for the past week. We all badly wanted to do well and show the rest of the world we had "hit the ground running in Durban", which had been Jack's theme since our tour to South Africa 12 months earlier. We now knew what to expect here and there were no excuses - but would we be able to do it?

England v Argentina

O ne of the problems today is that we are not kicking-off until 5pm. This is fine in terms of playing conditions and weather, far better than starting at 1pm or 3pm, but it is not our normal kick-off time back home, and although it's only an extra two hours in the day, it can ruin the players' routine.

I would normally expect to do a short morning kicking session at the ground between, say, 9.30 and 10.30, partly to fill in time, but more seriously to keep in the groove and get myself mentally and physically moving early in the day. Other players find they can stay in bed until late morning, but this does not work for me. We normally have an 11 o'clock backs' meeting separate from the forwards, who would be in the car park practicing yet more line-outs. We really should be pretty good at them by now!

However, the late kick-off allows an extra hour or so in bed and Rory and I are not awoken until 10 am by our alarm call, a luxury very rarely experienced these days, especially at home with two young children. Rory also has two girls, Rebecca and Alexandra. I'm Godfather to Alexandra, and we both value the extra rest we have had in the last seven days.

Dave and I planned an 11 o'clock drill at the stadium as the backs are not meeting until 1pm. So after my standard breakfast of cornflakes and toast, washed down by orange juice, tea or coffee, we are ready for the off in our World Cup mini-bus with Calvin and Cassie, our two Durban-based Police Officers. This morning I am joined again by JC and Catty, who are both getting into the swing of kicking on the morning of matches, although I'm sure an element of this is just filling in time before the kick-off.

This morning's session very nearly took place on the training pitch as we came across a groundsman, not dissimilar to many in England, who on the morning of the game feel that it is far too difficult to allow a couple of players onto the pitch because they have too much work to do on the ground. After a short discussion he allowed us onto the dead ball area, although from what I could see the lines were already painted, the grass cut and no more preparation was needed. The truth is that someone failed to inform him that we were coming and being the master of his own territory he was going to flex his muscles. Funny how they seem to be sensitive the world over. All's well that ends well and we did our business and set off back to the hotel.

The build-up had started yet we still had over five hours to kick-off. A pasta lunch was followed by the one o'clock meeting in the team room, which coincided with the kick-off of the Western Samoa-Italy game in East London, of significant interest to us because they were our next Pool opponents. The backs' meeting somehow got lost in the activity of watching this game and we never did get round to discussing what we planned to do this afternoon. We were able to sit and watch the whole game, an entertaining match well won by the Samoans who showed that they will be a big threat to us next Sunday. However, it's not the best preparation for a difficult international match and at three o'clock, just as we were gathering before departing to the ground, the Wales-Japan game was also kicking off and minds were wandering once more. Finally, Will switched off the television and we headed down from our second floor team room to the waiting coach. Wales went on to have a comfortable 55-5 victory over the Japanese to get the reign of Alec Evans off to a successful start.

By now the hotel was filling up with our supporters who started to arrive from England the day before to follow us through our World Cup campaign. Leaving the hotel to raptures of "Swing Low Sweet Chariot" reminded us how important this was to a lot of people and just how many had made the long trip to South Africa. The stadium, which holds 50,000 people, was nowhere near capacity, although a crowd of 30,000 was expected with several groups of very partisan supporters spread around the ground.

Sara had arrived with Emily, Beth and Michael, and I had spoken to her briefly. Having not had the easiest of overnight flights with two young children, she was feeling a little bit under the weather. But she was pleased to be in Durban and looking forward to an entertaining match, a handsome victory and a happy reunion, as were many other wives and girlfriends who were on the same flight.

The build-up to a big match is different for every player. Often in club games the captain will get the whole team out on the pitch to do a series of warm-up exercises and ball handling drills, although I have never seen this happen with an international side. Forwards generally like to take their time and get changed reasonably slowly, getting bandaged up and rubbed down by the physio and masseur. Several of the backs, on the other hand, like to get changed reasonably quickly to start the stretching exercises and some light jogging indoors if possible. At Twickenham there is an area adjoining the main England dressing room where there is room to do exercising, stretching and even a kicking net. A similar facility is available in Durban. I like to get out on the pitch early to do a few passing and kicking drills, and to wander around checking the strength and prevailing direction of any winds which will affect both kicking out of hand and off the ground. I also like to have a couple of strikes at goal-kicks so the first one in the game will not be the first I've taken for some time. I tend to use a drill which kicks a ball up the try line with the aim of hitting the near upright. Whether I hit it, or how close I get to the post, intends to have an impact on how the kicking is going to go. I remember against Scotland, in the last game of the Five Nations championship, having two kicks, hitting the near post and then the far post, and thinking that would do. I went on to kick seven out of eight. Today I did not strike either post, although after five or six attempts I felt reasonably comfortable that I was striking the ball well and the line was pretty straight.

There was rain in the air. As we practiced earlier in the morning there had been a couple of heavy showers and now just before kick-off it was again raining heavily. After all the perfect conditions we have seen the other games played in, isn't it typical that it is raining for our opening match. However, by kick-off the rain had stopped and it did not return during the match.

Unfortunately, our performance was riddled with mistakes and was one of the poorest showings I can remember from an England team for several years. We got no rhythm into the game or established any great platform from which to build attacks, and the physical threat from the Argentinians in the scrum and the loose caused a lot of problems. It was almost as if we were coasting and no-one could shake themselves free from the apathy. Strange you may think for players in an England shirt performing this way, but I can assure you that strenuous efforts were made to get the boys to snap out of this state of mind.

We had taken an early lead with a couple of penalties, while the Argentinians were missing them at the other end, and although it was a reasonably solid start, neither side was gaining any ascendancy. Our game recently has been built on good first phase possession,. This provides a platform to get our backs and forwards running against the opposition in a combined fashion, with inter-passing between the two, producing sustained pressure and several stages of possession, ultimately leading to the opposition running out of defenders and room being created for our strike runners and finishers out wide. If this breaks down, however, and we cannot gain any continuity, the game becomes a stultified affair of set pieces and kicks at goal, neither very entertaining to play in or watch. And this, unfortunately, is what happened in this game. Even when we were able to get some good possession and try to mount attacks we were guilty of making basic handling errors which gave the ball back to the opposition.

As the game wore on the Argentinians became more confident and they obviously felt they could steal a surprise victory against England. Indeed, the neutrals in the 30,000 crowd, having started on our side, could sense an upset and were cheering for the Argentinians by the end of the game. We let an 18-3 lead dwindle down to a final score of 24-18, with our opponents finishing the stronger of the two sides. We ended up with Skipper Will Carling leaving the field with a badly bruised ankle and a side that had lost its shape and form, desperately hanging on to a vital victory which at least meant our World Cup chances had not been blown up in the first

Swapping shirts after our disappointing opening game against Argentina.

encounter. My six out of six penalty goals and two drop goals from two attempts proved the wisdom of the excessive practice we had put in during the week leading up to this game. As we never really looked like scoring a try, this gave us a victory we possibly only just deserved, although it could have easily alluded us in the closing minutes.

The atmosphere in the dressing room was very muted, almost as if we had lost. The team was gripped by tension and fear, very similar to the opening game in the 1991 World Cup, against the then holders New Zealand when we also froze on the big day on our own ground. This should not have been the case again and something was clearly wrong. The forwards complained they were very tired after such a physical confrontation with the Argentinians, particularly in the scrum. The dressing room was littered with bodies lying on their backs with their legs up against the wall trying to remove the lactic acid from tired limbs. Will was in serious distress with his ankle injury caused by some over-robust Argentinian rucking, and was clearly in doubt for the Italy game on Wednesday. I was drafted into the press conference with Jack to explain our performance, which was not easy, and there were some obviously very disappointed English journalists as well as players. No doubt we would get a mauling from the papers back home, but on this occasion it would be thoroughly deserved.

The only thing to look forward to was a reunion in hospitality box number 604 with Sara, Emily and Beth, and I couldn't wait to get up there. It is on these occasions when the attention of a four year-old, not too bothered about the intricacies of World Cup qualification, is really welcome. Beth was even less interested - being fast asleep and shattered after an eventful 36 hours. Sara fortunately realised the seriousness of the situation, but also knew that to win a game like this is a million times better than losing it.

Will disappeared back to the hotel immediately for treatment and I stepped into the breach at the after-match reception to pass on my congratulations to the Argentinian team. For them it was a wonderful performance and one which if reproduced would stand them in good stead for their remaining two Pool games, against Western Samoa and Italy, and perhaps see them qualify for the quarter-finals. As for England, we had a lot of work to do. We were a very proud squad and would bounce back. When Jack had asked us to "hit the ground running" in Durban, he had not expected it to be backwards.

Sunday, May 28th

The morning after the day before is not a pleasant experience after such a poor team performance. I have not witnessed such a lack-lustre showing for many a year, and as I said at the press conference, it was almost a throwback to the 1980s. The only good thing on this Sunday morning is that I do not have a hangover from the excesses of the previous evening. One thing about playing three games in a week in the World Cup is that you cannot go mad the night after a game, which rugby players have been known to do on the odd occasion. So I was up early with a clear head and not feeling too tired, as it was one of those international matches which had not been too physically demanding on the backs because of its stop-start nature. Clearly, however, the forwards were in a much worse state.

I had a couple of interviews to carry out, including speaking to David Hands to pen my column for *The Times* for the Monday morning in which I tried to explain why we turned in such a poor performance. Paralysis by analysis can often be the case after a performance such as this, but even so there was a lot of talking to do, mostly to make people feel that we have found the solution to the problem. I am not sure in this case we would necessarily find the solution, and I'm not one for dwelling too much on the ifs and buts of such a situation. Talking privately with Jerry Guscott later in the day, he believes that not only were the players thinking about the quarter-finals, but they also had half a mind on the final, following the overhype in England before we left for South Africa.

Will and I, and one or two others, made a conscious decision during the season to be positive about the World Cup and to state clearly that we were going to South Africa to win it. All the squad has to really believe this deep down. We thought this would help our campaign, because without a deep-seated belief that we were good enough to beat the other sides in the world, we didn't think we could ever conquer the opposition. This view had caught on in England following the Grand Slam, and perhaps the hype was too much for a lot of the players to control.

Perhaps we would look back on yesterday and view it as a blessing in disguise, which ultimately spurs us on to greater things. I am a great believer in being confident and positive in our ability, but the odd kick up the pants now and again does nobody any harm. We had certainly received one almighty boot up the rear end.

After finishing my explanation to *The Times* readers, we had a rendezvous at 10 am for a light post-match training session at a local gym and health club, designed to take away the aches and pains and mental scars from yesterday evening. This was not a strenuous session, more for recovery purposes, bearing in mind that in three days our second international is taking place. The boys' spirits on these occasions are usually raised fairly quickly, especially when Ben Clarke finds himself pushed fully clothed into the swimming pool on arrival. The aim was for a bit of lighthearted fun allied to some stretching and light training.

Dave Alred was put in charge of the swimming pool where we underwent several lengths of arm only and leg only swimming to stretch the muscles. Others were to be found upstairs in the gym on a varying assortment of rowing, jogging and cycling machines. Any excuse to sit down and watch TV while pretending to get a sweat on early on a Sunday morning was the choice of most. Dewi Morris and Damian Hopley were spotted in the children's paddling pool, lying horizontal in the warm water. Nobody quite got to the bottom of their training programme! However, it was a fun morning, good for team spirit and moral was rising once again. Swimming not being my strongest subject at school, I managed a few lengths before retiring to the rowing machine for a gentle outing, and then with "Smurf" decided it was time for a cup of coffee in the club bar.

Over in the corner was the management trio of Jack, Les and the Skipper in serious conversation. Jack called me over, dismissed poor old "Smurf" and said: "We've got a challenge for you. Are you're up to it?" Jack was forever putting out challenges to the squad, since he took over in May 1994. My challenge was to lead the side against Italy in our second Pool game as Will was definitely sitting this one out. It was only the second time I had been asked to captain England, having filled Will's boots in 1989 in Romania when shin splits kept him out of the team. I was hoping we could repeat that performance when we beat the Romanians 58-3 in Bucharest, a score which still stands

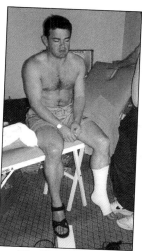

The Skipper receives treatment for his badly bruised ankle.

as the record England margin of victory. I would settle for much less than this against Italy. A victory with a much improved team performance will do.

Jack had some strong things to say about the performance privately to Will and I, and in particular about that of certain individuals. He was worried about the make-up of the team and the state of mind of the squad. He was especially concerned about the performance of the forwards. I have said it before, and I will say it again, international rugby is won and lost by forwards. Backs generally can only lose international rugby matches; they only assist the forwards in winning them. Without a good forward performance, backs are unlikely to win a game on their own, certainly not at the highest level. Before coming to South Africa we thought we had a pack of forwards capable of taking on anyone in the world when they are in the mood. But we had to get them in the mood more often and more consistently. There was still a tendency on occasions to drift into games where nobody was taking the initiative or responsibility to get things going, almost giving the impression they were not interested. Nobody ever goes onto the international field with this in mind, but sometimes the poor level of performance can give this impression. I am sure a lot of our supporters sat in England watching their early Saturday evening television were disappointed with our performance and by what appeared, from a distance, to be a lack of pride and passion in the England jersey.

What would Jack do to give the side a shake-up? This is where the art of good management comes in as the balance needs to be found between the use of the carrot and the stick. In terms of selection, too much carrot and the team becomes complacent. The players don't feel they are under enough pressure to perform. Too much stick and players are constantly feeling threatened, thereby inhibiting their performances. Either way the team performance suffers. The key is to keep the edge to a settled and successful group of players who have confidence in each other's ability, and who do not feel they are constantly under the threat of being dropped. Sometimes, though, the manager has to reassess the situation and maybe a dose of the short-sharp-shock therapy is required. Perhaps we need a little bit of this to re-focus one or two minds.

We discussed for half an hour the make-up of the team to play Italy and looked for ways of explaining yesterday's performance. I was pleased to have been given the opportunity to captain the side in the World Cup, albeit only as a stand-in on a temporary basis for Will, who would obviously be back for the Western Samoa game. But it was something I was looking forward to and I felt an important job had to be done to get the team back on the tracks.

Time now to get away from the pressure of international rugby and into relaxation mode. I agreed to meet Sara, Michael and the children at our hotel at lunchtime so I could switch off and spend some time with the family. I have always found it important to be able to switch between focusing totally on the rugby job in hand, and what is needed for the next game, and using relaxation time to full effect so you do not burn yourself out. I think this is what has happened to the squad in the last ten days as we have been couped up together thinking only about the World Cup. Some players find it difficult when there is not the work distraction which fills the majority of their time at home. It is important to compartmentalise the different facets and have the ability to switch on and off quickly. I realise this may not be possible for everybody, but it is obviously an unhealthy state of mind to think of nothing but the next game for ten days. You can become stale over such a period and this may be one of the many reasons why we performed so badly against Argentina. Most of us had been ready to play the game on the previous Tuesday. Mentally we probably found it difficult to maintain the level of readiness through until the Saturday. For the Italy game, the problem is probably the reverse in that we only have three days to switch on, although I think we will be better because of this.

A relaxing Sunday afternoon on the beach beckoned, but trying to force Emily to eat some of her lunch amid the excitement of Daddy building sandcastles and running in and out of the waves was not easy. One of the great things about Durban at this time of the year is that the weather is not too hot or humid. By English standards, these are almost perfect summer days for the children to be playing on the beach. So off we trotted *en famille* to enjoy the many miles of Durban sand. First, of course, we had to buy a bucket and spade for Daddy to do his digging. Like most children, Emily loves the seaside and no doubt in due course her eight-week-old sister Beth will follow suit. We lived in France for a year in 1992 when I was playing for Toulouse and spent a great deal of that summer either on the Mediterranean or Atlantic coasts of South Western France. Emily, as a then two-year old, has happy memories of her time at the seaside. She was soon telling me how much she liked South Africa. Sara realises she may not see a great deal of me, bearing in mind our first priority, but we both appreciated the time that we were together, as did the boys whose loved ones had also arrived. Some of the old school may not approve of wives and girlfriends on a rugby tour, particularly the World Cup, although I strongly believe if it is handled properly, and both the players and wives/girlfriends are sensible about it, it can prove just the antidote we need to the intensity of the rugby.

By the time we met again at 6.30 there was a more relaxed mood to the party. Brian gave his views on the forward performance, and Jack pencilled in his team for Wednesday and asked us to sleep on it until the following morning when he would announce it to the rest of the team. The squad meeting that evening was an open forum, or what we like to call our honesty session, where players can be openly critical knowing it will not go any further. After discussion with the management on yesterday's game, we had a players' only meeting which Will often calls so we can be even more honest and self critical. The good thing about these meetings is that some of the more junior members of the squad, who may otherwise feel intimidated, can say their piece. Richard West, the Gloucester second row who was uncapped and the most inexperienced member of the squad, thought people were distracted by everything else that was going on associated with the World Cup, particularly watching all the other matches, which is not the usual routine in the build-up to Five Nations. At home we have only our next opponent to focus on. Here there are many other matches and teams to watch and become obsessed by. Clearly, this is not healthy. It is important not to get too paranoid about things, but the air has to be cleared, and this was being achieved this evening.

Monday, May 29th

With the competition now well under way, there is not too much time to kill. We have only two days before our next match against Italy when a victory will almost certainly give us qualification into the quarter-finals. Two days, of course, is less than the normal time we have for a Five Nations preparation, and so there will be little excuse that time will drag.

Jack has called a 10 o'clock meeting to go through the tactics for the Italy game, but more importantly to announce the team at a press conference. We are also training today at King's Park under lights at 5pm, as this again will be the kick-off time. To pack as much into the day as possible, especially with Sara and the family being here, I decided to waste no time and do an extra early morning kicking session with Dave, starting at 8.30 after the usual light breakfast.

Many of the boys seem to have found the last few days a bit of a drag. Fortunately, I am able to find many different ways to occupy my time, either on rugby business or leisure. Rarely do I find myself lounging around the hotel or cat-napping in the afternoon, which an awful lot of players do. Phil de Glanville made a good point in one of our team meetings that players were becoming a little bit lethargic because of all the extra sleep they were getting and were not as active as they were back home. Perhaps there was also an argument that we should be doing more together as a squad in our leisure time. So this week it was decided that one or two more activities would be organised to get players into the routine of doing things. At home most players are rushing around at 100 miles an hour and often find their minds are not too over-focused on rugby. We have to guard against people becoming lazy in their day-to-day lifestyle on a tour of this nature, because there is a danger of this lethargy being transferred onto the field.

Still, there is no fear of that for me with a workaholic kicking coach and at 8.30 we were round the back of the hotel on the opposition's training pitch. There wasn't much chance of the Italians being on the field so early in the morning. David Norrie, of the *News of The World*, had decided to do a feature on our kicking practices and the successes we have had over the last 18 months. He was also interested in trying out the Adidas Predator boot we had been using for the last six months to see if Dave could work his magic on him. We agreed that David and his photographer could turn up at 9.30 after we had done our hour. I have never found early-morning training particularly easy or enjoyable, although these beautiful conditions make it much more pleasant compared with some of the cold, windy, wet and even snowy conditions back in the UK. We concentrated this morning purely on contact with very little run-up, focusing solely on what we call "hard foot", trying to transmit as much power as possible through the foot without using too much leg action. By 9.30 we were ready for the snappers. Unfortunately, Norrie decided on his second kick, with me holding the ball, to take most the ground with him and did some serious damage to his thigh. This meant the cancellation of any future sessions and one very upset press man disappeared for treatment.

At 10 o'clock Jack announced the team to play Italy and it contained the rather unusual but brave decision to move Jason Leonard from the loosehead to the tighthead and give a first full cap to Graham Rowntree, of Leicester. "Wiggy", as he is affectionately known, has worked hard for the last 18 months, and although he came on as a temporary replacement for Jason earlier in the season, he has never been selected as a first choice. Picking him on the loosehead side would provide some impetus into our forwards' running game and moving Jason over to the tighthead clearly sent a big message to Victor that he was under a lot of pressure for his place.

The second rows were kept the same, Jonners and Bayf, and in the back row there was also the inclusion of Neil Back on the open side to partner Ben Clarke and Tim Rodber. Rodders was still struggling a little bit with his game, but he has been one of our outstanding back row forwards in the last 12 months. It was felt that he and Clarkey needed another run as soon as possible. In the continued absence of Deano, whose hamstring is still trouble-some, The Pitbull will lead the forwards, and Jack felt this was a sufficiently strong pack to beat Italy. In the backs there were two enforced changes, with Kyran returning to see what he could do in place of Dewi, and Phil de Glanville taking over from Will. Jerry in the cen-tre, and the Underwood brothers and Mike Catt, completed the team. It was announced that I would be leading the side and that we would train at 5pm today. Otherwise, there was not much to add other than for people to start to thinking about the way Italy played. As always, we had plenty of videos on our opposition, looking at their weaknesses and strengths. Recently, Italy had played some big matches, in particular against Ireland two weeks before we came out here, which they won 22-12. And although they lost 42-18 to Western Samoa, I thought they played pretty well in this game and were not worthy of such a heavy defeat. They would pose us certain problems but I was confident we would win the game.

Immediately following the announcement of the team, a press conference was held in the hotel for the hordes of British and local Press, as well as journalists from other parts of the world who follow the opposition teams. I was asked if there was a lot of pressure on England to pro-duce a much better performance and if, in fact, there was too much tension around. Obviously, I felt a better performance was needed, as recognised by the squad, and maybe there was a lot of tension, but much of this was caused by the unreal circumstances of the build-up. The World Cup is unique and a lot of players were still coming to terms with their surroundings. I was con-fident we would be able to raise our game, but at the same time we needed to enjoy ourselves and relax a bit more. It was important to concentrate on our own game rather than worry too much about the opposition. You always have to be aware of the opposition tactics and spend some time analysing the way they play, but you can sometimes overplay this and it is more important to make sure your own game is in order and that you are taking the game to them,

rather than waiting for them to do things. This is what we had done against Argentina and against Italy we needed to impose our game on them. When England do this at their best, as we have proved in the past two years, there are few sides in the world capable of liv-ing with us. We keep recalling the first 20 minutes against South Africa in Pretoria in June 1994. Obviously, 20 minutes now and again is not enough to win a World Cup, but we all know deep down we have the ability in the side if we can only pro-duce it.

Wiggy and Backy were clear-ly of interest to the media, and

Demonstrating the art of kicking to David Norrie, of the News of the World. But it ended in disaster...

they were submerged by the scribes after the press conference. Both had been given a big opportunity to prove themselves in South Africa, especially Backy who had played for England previously, but was constantly living under the threat of being too small for international rugby, although week in, week out he produces the most consistent performances of any back row forward in the UK. I was confident he would perform well against Italy.

More time to be a family man for the next couple of hours, most of it being spent buried in the Durban sands by Emily who found it very amusing that Daddy should disappear totally and she would have to rescue me. There was no chance of me being unable to fill my time, especially this week with Emily and Beth in town, nor any danger of becoming too intense and over-focused on rugby. My life back in the UK is manic to say the least with work, family and rugby commitments. I have always found this a help when dealing with the pressures of international sport.

Training started well with myself and Dewi doing impersonations of Shaun Edwards, after being issued with shoulder pads. We have been told that these are illegal as far as International Board regulations go because they are not sewn into the jersey. However, they are being worn by every other side in the World Cup competition, and the administrators are doing nothing about this as they are clearly visible at the end of matches when teams change shirts. This was a bit of a novelty for us, and the majority of the backs thought it would be a good idea to impersonate rugby league and American footballers. We even had a game of six-a-side rugby league as part of the warm-up, which everybody seemed to enjoy. Certainly there were some big hits going in and even the odd swinging arm tackle, not unknown in rugby league. Dewi was the ideal man to explain all the rules, being one of our few northern-based players who has spent time this season training with Wigan, particularly with loose-forward Phil Carke. We spent the first 15 minutes coming short and practicing rugby league passes and the buzz we had generated continued into our normal session, which I thought was one of the best so far on tour. The players responded extremely well and in many ways Argentina had now been forgotten. We were now looking forward to the game against Italy. The goalkickers finished with their regular bout of post-training kicking, being left on our own with the security boys to do the fetching and carrying.

Part of the concentrated "in it together", as Jack keeps saying, started this evening with a visit next door to the local Japanese restaurant, which had been frequented by one or two of the lads last week. Tonight it was decided there would be a compulsory team outing and all 26 players, plus our two trusted security guards, Calvin and Steve, enjoyed a tasty Japanese steak dinner with the odd bottle of best South African red, selected exclusively by our resident wine expert from the *Today* newspaper, alias The Pitbull, who over the years appears to have gathered somewhat of a liking for the red nectar. A very pleasant, lighthearted evening was interrupted only by Terry Cooper, of the Press Association, who never lets up when he needs to speak to a player. He came into our private dinner to talk to Jason about moving over to tighthead prop for the Italy game. Not surprisingly, he was greeted with derision from the squad, and despite being given both yellow and red cards, which are carried at all times by the team to ward off undesirables whenever we are out socially and do not wish to be disturbed, Coops was not having any of this and had to be given a strong verbal reminder, which did not go down too well. He left under a cloud, but sometimes the press do not help themselves in these situations. We were not in the mood for discussing things with them.

It was reported back in the UK that this private dinner had been a "crisis session and honesty meeting" for the players to explain why we had played so badly on Saturday and what we were going to do about it. This could not be further from the truth. It was a very relaxed, enjoyable evening. We save our honesty meetings for other occasions. This was yet another case of the press looking for a story and making something out of nothing. The Scots had suffered a similar fate earlier last week when they had been accused of causing some damage in a restaurant, which they rigorously denied. This is just some of the small things you have to put up with in the public spotlight.

Tuesday, May 30th

T he phone went at 8.30 and I expected it to be the early morning call as we were meeting at 10 o'clock to go for training, our last light run-out before the Italy match. I was surprised to hear it was the manager asking if he could see me in his room in ten minutes.

Jack is renowned for his late-night and early-morning management meetings. He was sat in the living room of his suite going over the training session for this morning which he wanted to discuss with me. On the day before a game we had become accustomed to the final training session being run by Will, or the captain for the day. As Will had not missed many games for seven years, this was nearly always him. However, as I was leading the troops tomorrow Jack felt that I should know what he had in mind.

It is important for the captain to have some authority with the team he is leading, even though it may be only on a temporary basis. Will had said to me yesterday that he would take a back seat for the next 48 hours so I could effectively take over the XV that would take the field. Jack was concerned that this was not quite the normal build-up to an international, having only had two sessions to prepare, and there were a few extra things he wanted to go over in training this morning, rather than the normal light run-out.

There were certain bits of defensive work he wanted to concentrate on, especially the kicking of Diego Dominguez, the talented Italian fly-half who had also been capped for Argentina and was clearly one of their best players. He was also concerned about their line-out patterns, particularly the long throws over the back to the centre or flanker coming up into midfield to take the ball. Again our spy in the Italian camp had been Austin Swain, our "Spook", also a rugby man in his own right who understood how rugby players operated. It was clear that they were also spying on us, and they had been practicing defending the short sides, which we had been working on. There was obviously a lot of undercover work going on in this World Cup.

I was a bit concerned that the session would go on for too long, which I felt was unnecessary as we had trained very well yesterday. We were accustomed to a short, sharp final session the day before a game, and I wanted to stick close to this tested pattern. We had moved away from this for the Argentina game and several of the players, particularly the forwards, were unhappy that the routine had been broken. I wanted to get as close to normal this time round. Unfortunately, as with a lot of our training sessions, I felt we went on a little bit too long and the session finished on a low note rather than on a high tempo as yesterday. It is often difficult to keep the balance exactly right, but there is a danger of going on too long to a point where the session deteriorates and little productive work is carried out.

Otherwise, the day before the game was a low-key affair with a couple of hours with the family over lunch, followed by the extra kicking session at three o'clock, again in the stadium. We like to go through our session of 33 kicks the day before a game when I sometimes find it difficult to get my kicking together. I complained to Dave that we had been doing too much kicking, although maybe this was just an excuse for what had started well but had deteriorated into a poor session. We have done more kicking in the last two weeks than ever before and sometimes the day before a game there are a lot of other things going through

Relaxed and happy in training before the tournament gets under way...

Raring to go - the boys pictured outside the Sunnyside Park Hotel in Johannesburg.

Taking it easy on one of the interminable coach journeys while the Skipper catches up on his sleep.

Rory wades into the inevitable signing session before we leave.

The Wasps connection - pictured with my clubmate and Ireland prop Nick Popplewell before leaving Heathrow.

Manager Jack Rowell - as always he pushed us to the limit in training.

In it together - on our way to some recreational paint balling.

Spreading the good news - Will Carling on his Cellnet after our victory over the Aussies.
Inset: The Barmy Army demonstrate their support for the Skipper.

Nursing our injuries - Kyran Bracken, myself and Rory Underwood getting the full treatment.

The smiles say it all - Will and Rory join me in the dressing room celebrations after dumping the world champions.

Me and my old pal Dewi.

Proud to be English - me and Tony Underwood belt out the National Anthem.

Escaping the clutches of Argentinian Federico Mendez with Ben Clarke in attendance.

On top of the world - Rodders and Johnners on Table Mountain.

Baywatch it ain't - Rory, Phil de Glanville, Tony and Kyran in the Durban surf.

Lining up a putt on the 18th green at the Royal Durban Golf Club.

The Big One! This is when all those extra hours of kicking training paid off.

It's tense on the bench - Jack with his assistant John Elliott.

Doing the social rounds: above - Kyran, Neil Back and Ben Clarke manage a smile at the opening gathering; right - Jason Leonard wears the badge reserved for Nelson Mandela; and (below) the two Underwood brothers pretend they're enjoying themselves.

Training in the midday sun.

Daddy builds a sandcastle with the help of Emily.

Dining out with Sara and baby Beth.

At least Beth stayed awake for this shot with big sister Emily.

The look says it all - it's all over.

your mind and yet the adrenalin is not really pumping, so mentally it becomes much harder to keep everything on line. The actual scores in the 33 kicks were not very good and we finished by doing five kicks from 45 yards out in front, not part of the original exercise, but it allowed me to get the contact feel back by the end of the session. All round, we found it a useful afternoon, although Dave recognised I was mentally quite tired and that there were other things on my mind apart from goalkicking.

It has often been said that being a fly-half, goalkicker and captain can put too much responsibility on a player and I think it is true that there have been many instances when this has seemed to be the case. At fly-half you have a lot of decision making and there is extra pressure as a goalkicker. Throw in the captaincy as well and it can cause problems. I was not particularly worried about this for the game tomorrow, as I felt the kicking was going well enough and I had a technique on which I could rely. I was not feeling overburdened by the captaincy, as I had no intention of changing anything from the routine that the team had gone through for the past few years with Will in charge. Dave was concerned about whether I could key in quickly enough to my goalkicking mode when a penalty or conversion was needed.

The seven o'clock team meeting, chaired by Jack and myself, was very positive. Jack tends to go through a routine of the basics which players need to carry out to be successful in international rugby. As in most international sports, you can never go over the basics required to win such matches too often in the same way, although it may be repetitive, you can never do too much of the basic skills required, albeit that it is far more interesting if you have variations to the training. In the build-up to a game, Jack likes to concentrate on the positive side of our play, discussing specifics like scrum attack and defence, line-out attack and defence, kicking strategy, pressure on their ball, backs supporting backs, etc.

He often talks about specific items, rather than speaking generally, which does not allow players to build up a picture of what is actually needed. We also finish the session by

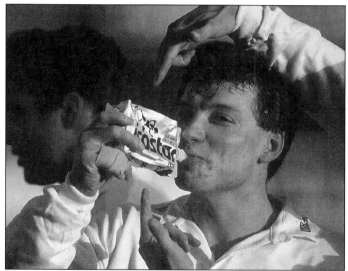

Taking refreshment during training.

talking through on the blackboard the general game plan we want to adopt from various positions on the field. This is something we used to do an awful lot more in the early days of England's success when we went back to square one and almost re-invented the wheel. Since then the players have a much better idea of what we are trying to do. You can never become too structured in what you are trying to do, although England have certainly been criticised because of this in the past. You definitely need a framework in which to operate so that the team has some base from which to work, especially if things are going wrong and you are struggling to put your game together. You need to have something to fall back on.

I entered the team dinner that evening feeling that our build-up had been more normal and that there was a mood which suggested we were more comfortable in our surroundings. Although it would be a tough game tomorrow, it would be tougher for the Italians.

England v Italy

We have the luxury of a lie-in this morning as kick-off is not until 5pm. I want to try and replicate the day as much as possible to that of a Five Nations match back home with a 3pm kick-off, which would mean trying to move everything back a couple of hours during the day.

Normally at home I would do a kicking session at about 9 am after an early breakfast, but this morning Rory and I were not woken by the alarm until 9.30. This would give me time to do a kicking session at the ground at 11 o'clock before returning for a backs' meeting, followed by the team gathering. Hopefully, the day would not drag too much.

We managed to sweettalk the groundsman at King's Park into letting us on to the main pitch. He was reluctant to do this before the Argentina game, but it is amazing what the promise of an England shirt can do. This was not a very long session and would do little damage to the playing surface, which is in magnificent condition. Most of the manicuring had been done and there is no reason why the kickers should not be allowed on the pitch on the morning of the game. This is more of a problem with the touchy groundsmen in the Northern Hemisphere than it is in the Southern Hemisphere where often they play curtain raisers before the main game. It had been agreed that this would not be the case in the World Cup, which had disappointed the South Africans, who were used to seeing two or three games on matchdays.

Jim Rosenthal and his trusted cameraman, OD, followed us to King's Park this morning to get some footage of the pre-match preparation I go through. They obviously have a job to do and they know when to be around and when to leave us alone. I think they are interested in the routines we go through and why this is necessary.

In a short session, kicks are taken from very narrow angles only two or three yards from the try-line on either side of the posts, which gives you virtually nothing to aim at, but is very good for disciplining the kicking style into straight lines with the hope that when you go on the field the target you are aiming for appears so big compared to the one you had in your mind earlier in the day. Also, on the morning of an international there is far more adrenalin flowing and everything seems to be working in better order than the previous afternoon. We only spend about 20 minutes actually kicking and when we feel happy with the contact the session comes to an end. Then I like to finish with a few drop goals, taken after receiving a pass, just in case they come in useful at some stage of the game. It has been known for the odd late drop goal to win a match. A short interview followed with Jim Rosenthal when he asked about the mood of the team and whether I had a message for our many supporters back home. I hoped they would see a much improved England performance this afternoon and one they recognised to be from the true England side and not another disappointing performance as seen on Saturday. I was convinced we would put up a better show.

On returning to the hotel we had our normal backs' meeting at which Les Cusworth and Will usually go through a few issues. Will was obviously not around for this game and we concentrated on one or two areas we felt would be important. Firstly, we wanted to run aggressively with the ball in hand when we were trying to attack the gain line and set targets for the back-row forwards to hit, while trying to keep our depth when we decided to take the ball wide to make room for Tony and Rory to show their speed. Secondly, we felt consistently in

training in the last fortnight that we had been getting too flat when trying to take the ball wide.
This was being doubly compounded by the
quick, aggressive defences we had already seen,
giving no room in the centres for any great cre-
ativity. We needed to by-pass the midfield area
and get the ball wide without putting ourselves
under too much pressure. Thirdly, we also wanted to attack the short side, with Mike Catt in particular taking the ball direct from Kyran Bracken
when we were able to get into midfield and give
ourselves the option to attack on two sides of
the pitch. If the Italians proved that they had
sorted out their defence on the short side, we
felt this would leave holes elsewhere which we
needed to exploit.

Our two wingers were given the specific task
of feeding in as much information as possible to
the half-backs as regards short-side defences so
we could make reasoned decisions about where
to attack. In the heat of the battle, split second
decisions are taken and it is very important to
have as much information as possible to help
the half-backs make these all-important decisions. All in all the backs felt good about the
game and were looking forward to playing
with confidence and having a go at our Italian
opposite numbers to show them what we are
capable of doing. Although the forwards win
and lose international rugby matches, I believe
the backs can set the tone by the way they

Directing operations against Italy.

start the game, both by being aggressive in defence and direct in attack, which gives the forwards the targets to hit. This also allows the forwards to get into the game early on. If we
become loose and make mistakes, it has a very negative effect on the forwards' morale. As
their name suggests, forwards like going forward and are not keen on their backs going backwards and putting the team in trouble. We were still searching for this elusive continuity
between backs and forwards.

In the team meeting I suggested to Jack that we just have ten minutes with the XV selected players, rather than the whole squad. Although it is important in a World Cup campaign
to be a team of 26 and try to involve everybody, I did feel for this game it was crucial that
the XV taking the field were as one and that we spent a bit of time together. The rest of the
squad and management left the team room and Jack and I had our few last words. I wanted to reiterate the importance of this game and how nothing any more in international rugby
could be taken for granted, even though many people back home were under the impression
that Argentina, Italy and Western Samoa was an easy group. This is not the case. We had set
ourselves high standards in the last five years, but against Argentina we had slipped from
those standards. There were a lot of players in the team with good international reputations
which could soon be ruined by a string of poor performances. There were also one or two
younger players who were trying to make a name for themselves and they had to start taking more responsibility. We felt there had been a few people hiding on Saturday and success
at international level could not be achieved if that was the case. We had proved to ourselves

that we were not a team that bottled on the big occasion. We clearly needed to convince ourselves, our supporters and the rest of the World Cup participants that we were here to do business and it was about time we started to show it. The team was ready and we were looking forward to getting stuck into the Italians.

The coach trip to any big game is always rather tense. Very few people crack jokes, most of them being in their own little worlds, either staring out of the window or oblivious to the surroundings with the earphones blasting out their favourite melodies. I'm generally a sitter and watcher on these occasions. A bigger crowd of over 30,000 was expected today as there were more supporters arriving all the time.

In the warm-up I wanted to get the backs and back-row out onto the field before kick-off to go through some stretching exercises and handling drills to sharpen up their reactions. Some players, particularly Deano and The Pitbull, are unhappy about warming up on the pitch before big games, having spent years in their routines inside the dressing room away from any prying eyes. I always prefer to spend some time on the pitch, getting used to the surroundings and warming up like we do for a training session. I sometimes think we spend more time warming up for training than we do for the actual matches that start at a very hectic pace. Many club sides in England now collectively warm up on the pitch and go through a rigorous routine of stretching, ball handling and running. I wanted to try and instill some of this into the backs in particularly.

The front five tend to have their own peculiar ways of getting ready for an international and the forwards often have their own private meeting in the dressing room about 15 minutes before kick-off to prepare themselves mentally for the physical conflict about to start, which is much tougher than that for which the backs have to prepare. The warm-up went smoothly and I did a bit of kicking practice down the touchline, hitting the post once, a good sign. I also managed to win the toss with Massimo Cuttitta, the Italian prop forward and captain, after shaking hands with the Irishman Stephen Hilditch, the referee for the day and one of the world's most respected officials in whom we have a lot of confidence. Then, with about five minutes to go, the infamous black cloud appeared from the sea and soaked King's Park, just as it had done on Saturday before kick-off against Argentina. Why is it that here we are in South Africa, in perfect rugby playing conditions, and our pitch gets drenched just before kick-off? The South Africans said it was to make us feel at home, but we are much happier playing in dry conditions and did not want to be made to feel we were back in England, thank you very much.

Despite the swirling wind coming in off the Indian Ocean, there did not appear to be any advantage from one end or the other, so having won the toss we decided to take the kick-off, allowing the opportunity to play into the opposition's half and put the pressure on immediately. We managed about five minutes of first-half play in the dry before the heavens opened again which made the ball very slippery. In those opening minutes we scored a good counter-attacking try from our own 22 on turning over a ball from the Italians, and generally started in a positive mood with players hungry to get in on the action. As the rain fell we started to make more mistakes, but we were the better side in the first half and were leading 16-3 a minute before half-time when Mike Catt unfortunately had a kick charged down, which led to a try and conversion, thereby closing the gap to 16-10 and giving the Italians hopes for the second half. Once again, however, we concentrated for 20 minutes and with an excellent try from Rory Underwood, we opened the gap to 27-10 before again finishing the game poorly with a last 10 minutes that can only be described as a shambles, allowing the Italians to close the gap to 27-20 with a try on the final whistle. We had still not produced the all-round performance we were looking for, but there were signs of improvement.

The press conference after the game concentrated on whether or not the England management was happy with the improvement and in which areas we thought we had done better. I don't think any of us were under the illusion that this was World Cup winning form, but we were on an upward curve and the victory enabled qualification for the quarter-finals following yesterday's win by Western Samoa over Argentina, coming back from a 26-10 deficit to win 32-26. Western Samoa and ourselves were through to the quarter-finals and our meeting on Sunday would now decide who were the winners of the Pool. We felt we had improved in piecing together our continuity game, although there were still far too many errors, especially in the ball retention department. However, there were still areas to improve on, especially the forwards' driving play and in creating space for the backs, who are obviously very dangerous when given a bit of room. But room is a precious commodity in this World Cup. Two good tries by the Underwood brothers proved that we have the finishing ability if only we can improve on the build-up work.

At the post-match reception I congratulated Italy on an excellence performance and on their improvement since the last World Cup, when they were also in our group, although we won comfortably 34-6. I suggested that maybe an expanded Five Nations championship to include Italy could be something the administrators would like to consider. And why not? They could be a very valuable addition to such a championship. I still feel we have to be constantly on our guard in the Northern Hemisphere about being too insular with our rugby, which will not help us in our battle against Southern Hemisphere supremacy. A thank-you to Steve Hilditch and his touch judges for their contribution, a few short words about the England performance and the traditional handover of ties and pins to the opposition captain ended my short speech and I was off for a brief reunion with Sara and the children before bidding them good night as the late kick-off meant we were getting close to Emily's bed time. A visit to one of the hospitality boxes for a quick drink, followed by a team barbecue and a couple of beers in the car park and it was time to leave King's Park for the second time in this World Cup, having played two, won two. As I mentioned in my after-match speech, we were already in a better position than we had been in 1991 when we had played one, lost one.

Time on the coach back to the hotel to reflect on the second round of matches played yesterday and today. The Western Somoa victory over Argentina was, of course, of particular interest to us. South Africa struggled to beat Romania 21-8, while France and Scotland had easy wins over the Ivory Coast and Tonga. Earlier today Australia had beaten Canada unconvincingly, and Ireland had thrashed Japan. New Zealand defeated a gallant Welsh team 34-9 in Johannesburg. The Welsh had been very confident of victory, but on the day did not have enough forward fire power. New Zealand are certainly looking the in-form team of the World Cup at the moment, despite South Africa's magnificent victory over the Aussies in the opening match. If we can win our group and overcome Australia in the quarter-finals, we may have to meet New Zealand in the semi's. It's starting to get interesting...

The glamour boys - Will and Jerry relax in the South African sun.

Thursday, June 1st

S ome of the English press have picked up on comments made in the Italy programme by David Campese, the Australian wing, who was quoted as saying that
the England team prays for sunshine but carries an umbrella. Campese said:
"Carling himself epitomises England's lack of skills. He has speed and strength but
plays like a castrated bull." They also added fuel to the fire with one of Campese's
quotes from the 1991 World Cup when he said: "Even if I had been born English, I
would never have wanted to play with such a conservative mob. Forget football. The
only thing you are likely to get on the end of an England back line is chilblains."

Obviously the love-hate relationship between Campo and the English team was going to
continue during this World Cup. I am looking forward to some more outbursts next week if
we beat Western Samoa and have to meet Australia in Cape Town. Campo seems to think he
has the God-given right to open his mouth and blast everyone in sight, however disrespectful
or disgraceful his comments might be. It's about time some of his views were shoved back
down his throat, as they were by the 1989 British Lions in the series which we won 2-1. He
is undoubtedly doing a fine job in firing up the English boys if we do meet them next week.
He certainly does not do himself or Australian rugby a great deal of justice. Even Bob Dwyer
has been quoted as saying Campese sometimes has a loose wire between his mouth and his
brain. There is also a rumour that he is as popular within his own squad as he is with the
England team. Still, if that's the way he wants to live his life, that's down to him. He has been
one of the world's greatest players, but judging by the way Peiter Hendriks went round him
in the opening game, he's not going to be the star of this competition.

After breakfast it was off for my favourite pastime, a spot of swimming at the La Lucia gym
and fitness club, just to the north of our Holiday Inn Hotel. I had picked up a bit of a dead
leg in the first ten minutes of last night's game and was therefore unable to do any running
or rowing , so I was thrust back into the swimming pool to loosen off my injury. Jack said at
the press conference that we had picked up one or two injuries against Italy and some of the
players were still carrying knocks from the Argentina game, which was starting to take their
toll. This may well have a reflection on the team to be picked to play Western Samoa on
Sunday. It would be difficult for some players to play three games in a week, particularly as
the Western Samoan clash is likely to be a very physical encounter. Jerry and Rory had also
picked up knocks against Italy and a few others were starting to go down with the dreaded
tummy bug, which tends to spread like wild fire throughout a squad as we virtually live on
top of each other. This is the last thing we want this week in the build-up to the Samoan
match. Jack will have some careful considerations to make in team selection.

The swimming proved very useful for my injury and although not the strongest swimmer I
enjoyed my 20 minutes of rehabilitation along with a couple of the forwards, Rodders and
Bayf, and my mate Rory who had seen me floundering in the school pool in 1974 when he
pulled me from the deep end. It is very useful to do some form of light recovery the day after
a game to prepare for training. I even had a wallow in the much warmer kiddies' pool at the
end of the session, followed by a relaxing coffee and bar of chocolate in the gym cafe. After
a few PR shots with the manager of the gym, we were back on the move.

A quick lunch in the hotel's burger restaurant with Sara, Emily and Beth, followed by an hour on the beach, was about all I could fit in with the family before we reconvened for more compulsory, collective social activity. It can be a little disappointing for Emily when Daddy turns up for an hour and then disappears again, but I will be able to see them later this evening at the Courage reception at the Durban Country Club. Sara was well aware before she came out here that the main business is to concentrate on the rugby and that we would see each other only sparingly. I think she was glad she came, although it's not that easy with two young children so far from home. Knowing Sara, she would have been more disappointed sitting at home this week instead of being in Durban. The weather was also improving and Emily was loving being on the beach all day .

At 2.30pm we met for a visit to the local War Games Society and a spot of paint balling. I'm not sure if Jack was aware of what we were up to, but if he had realised how dangerous this could be he would not have been so happy about the decision taken by the social committee, headed by Deano. I had heard a lot about paint balling as several of my work colleagues had been on excursions, and I was looking forward to it with a little trepidation. We were driven to what looked like a former small hospital, now derelict, on the edge of the harbour, a perfect setting for war games with small buildings adjoining the main house, surrounded by open grounds. The house was full of small rooms and staircases and it was even possible to get up on the roof. We were fitted out with safety masks and goggles and told we would each be given 20 or 30 rounds of Malteser-size, hard shell paint balls which explode on impact. Once shot, and therefore covered in a yellow or pink splodge of paint, you had to raise your gun and arms, shout you had been shot and return to base for a two-minute time-out.

We were warned to keep on the mask and goggles at all times until we returned to the safety zone. A blow in the eye with one of these paint balls could result in serious injury, if not indeed loss of sight, a serious repercussion, one would think, in the middle of a World Cup campaign. However, knowing the squad, it was a case of in for a penny, in for a pound, and once we were kitted out it was decided the backs would take on the forwards in the time honoured fashion.

The backs base camp was at one end of the garden, while the forwards were stationed in the far end of the building. The aim was to take the flag from the opposition camp while protecting your own flag. A siren signalled the start and end and we engaged in three battles to see who won the war. The vision of international rugby players diving for cover in the undergrowth and behind walls was a sight to behold. Being competitive and aggressive animals, the game soon deteriorated into an all-out battle with none of the rules being observed. Anyone who was foolish enough to come out of hiding with their arms up was making a big mistake. It was certainly painful if you were hit at close range.

I made one sortie deep into enemy territory, only to find my cover had disappeared under heavy fire and I was ambushed by a group of grisly forwards who took no pity on this puny fly-half. We also had our security officers joining us for the game to show us how it should be done, but even they were not to prove

Taking cover in our paint ball battle against the forwards

infallible against the might of the English pack. The sight of Deano, Bayf, Jason and The Pitbull launching a raid on the backs' camp was not a pretty one and had to be fought off with great bravery. Each game was broken up with shrieks, expletives and bursts of gunfire in what turned out to be an exhausting but very enjoyable afternoon. Several people took some heavy blows, including one of our security men who was bleeding profusely from the ear. Many had bruises to confirm their participation. The only disappointment was the absence of our Army man, known as "The Brigadier", otherwise Tim Rodber, who was claiming to be ill. We were convinced he was worried about taking on the cunning England back line and being embarrassed in the process. We managed to escape unscathed, apart from one or two flesh wounds.

We were back in time for the cocktail party hosted by Courage at the Durban Country Club. Sara had decided that Emily would stay in the hotel with Grandad for the evening, as it would be a bit late for her, and therefore turned up with some of the other wives and girlfriends at our hotel with only Beth in tow. The reception was being held for our sponsors and press, the venue being one of the top 30 golf clubs in the world where some of our boys had played last week. They had a strict no children rule, so you can imagine I had one or two problems when I arrived with Beth in arms. Although I managed to talk my way into the private room for the cocktail party, I was subsequently asked to leave, despite the fact that nine-week-old Beth was fast asleep and not really causing any problems. Not being ones to cause any fuss, Sara and I exited immediately to spend a quiet evening back at the hotel, the first time we had really been on our own this week. Several of the other players were disappointed that they did not have children to use as an excuse to leave the cocktail party. Although we know we have to attend, these events are not very inspiring and the players are only too pleased when they are over. Jane Guscott arrived late with six-week-old Holly and was also told she had to leave. Quite rightly, she refused as the players were leaving themselves in 15 minutes. Even if this was a club rule, this was a private function at which two young babies, not causing any trouble, should have been allowed to stay.

Sara and I had a pleasant private drink back at the hotel and waited for the others to return. A group of us decided to go next door to our favourite Japanese restaurant for dinner. We were joined by Jonathan and Gail Callard, who are expecting their first child in a few months time. Gail is probably the most nervous rugby wife I have ever met and finds its almost impossible to watch Jonathan play. Even at the Pilkington Cup Final she could not watch the game. Sarah had taken Emily and Beth to Twickenham, which did not work out because Beth was screaming and Emily did not want to sit in the stand, so Gail and Sara spent most of the game in the West Car Park playing with the children. Liz and Graham Dawe were also with us. Liz is probably one of the hardest done to rugby wives with Graham spending so many hours on the road travelling to training from his Launceston farm in Cornwall to Bath, about a three-hour drive, not to mention all the England sessions at Marlow. Selection for this World Cup is a great tribute to Dawsey, who was in the 1987 squad but missed out in 1991, having lost his place to John Olver, the Northampton hooker. But even at the age of 36, he has forced his way back into the squad and is, in fact, one of the fittest men in the team. I hope he gets a game along with JC in this World Cup.

It turned out to be a little bit of a Bath clique for dinner as we were also joined by Jerry and Jane Guscott, with little Holly, Phil de Glanville and fiancée Yolanda and Mike Catt with girlfriend Debbie, who is now living in the UK, but was back in his native South Africa. Despite having to take shifts in walking Beth around the restaurant, we had one of the most enjoyable evenings of the tour so far. We even managed to persuade Phil King, the Director in charge of ITV's operations out here, who was hosting his crew on the next table, to pick up the bill. Although a little cheeky, this was much appreciated.

The mood of the squad has improved significantly now we are two nil up and in the quarter-finals. Although we had an important big game coming up against Western Samoans, we had achieved our aim of getting to the quarter-final cut. As anticipated, South Africa or Australia still beckoned for the England team in ten days time.

Friday, June 2nd

The social committee had laid on a 5am alarm call for those who were interested in going out to see the shark nets laid out on the coast. Dewi was the only back who had the misfortune to set off on this trip. Most of the others had far more sense and stayed in bed.

Several of Deano's forward crew, including his Leicester team mates Wiggy and Johners, along with Clarkey, Neil Back, John Mallett and Graham Dawe, set off at the crack of dawn. The only slight problem was that just before leaving they were informed that only one shark had been caught in the last two months, and that the swell out of the harbour was in the region of four metres, not something you wanted to hear that early in the morning. However, there was no turning back and off they went with the ITV crew on board with intrepid interviewer Jim Rosenthal in hot pursuit of another story - but not one with a great deal of substance on this occasion. It later transpired that Phil King, ITV's World Cup producer, had been behind the whole trip to get an unusual angle for the viewers back home. Therefore, I didn't feel so bad for fleecing him for dinner the evening before. Not surprisingly, Deano managed to pick up "Dick of the Day" for getting so many people out of bed under false pretenses on what would have otherwise been a leisurely morning.

The more sensible members of the squad took up the offer of either a trip out to the Hugh Baiocchi Golf Club, some 30 miles north of Durban, also regarded as one of the world's finest, or a helicopter ride organised by our own RAF officer, Rory. He had managed to lay on a trip up the coast with the South African Air Force Squadron 15, based at Durban Airport, in one of their large troop helicopters. There was room for 16 of us and following a brief outline of the work carried out by Flight Officer Barske, we were loaded on board. This is the only helicopter squadron in the Natal region and they carry out a whole range of services for the Army and Police, as well as search and rescue missions on sea and land with the Drakensburg mountains not being too far away.

We were given a most enjoyable tour of the Durban coastline, past our hotel and the stadium, and up towards Umlanga Rocks and past the Beverly Hills Hotel, where we had hoped to be staying until the Rugby World Cup authorities decided otherwise. We flew at between 200 and 500 feet with the doors open we were able to see a party of wives and girlfriends enjoying the balcony of the Beverly Hills hotel overlooking the sea. Several of them had been invited there this morning to take part in the aerobic exercises of Mr Motivator on GMTV, who were screening much of their programme from South Africa this week to coincide with the World Cup. I think we were failing to appreciate the impact the competition was having back home. A quick sortie further up the coast and then inland and back across one of the large townships of Durban to the beach area and on past the harbour finished our exhilarating flight.

We were invited into the crew room for the usual military hospitality with tea and sandwiches Air Force style, and Rory felt very much at home. Not surprisingly, he took a little bit of stick from the boys about getting a real job, a bit rich coming from one or two of our semi-professional PR guys who don't seem to work too many long hours back in the UK these days. However, no names just yet... The helicopter and golf organisers were congratulated on their social activities, while Deano was still under pressure to explain his lack of shark expedition.

Training was scheduled for 8pm this evening to climatise to the kick-off time on Sunday, very late by English standards in that we rarely play night matches. The Skipper called a private backs kicking session at 3pm, having felt there was still some work to be done in this area following the Italy game, particularly with the back three on catching of high balls and clearing our lines. We have often maintained that one good clearance kick at a vital stage of a big game could save or cost us continued involvement in this World Cup.

The golfers were in trouble because they were late back, which, quite rightly, did not go down well with the Skipper, who had already agreed to delay the kicking session by an hour to allow them to finish their game. Team discipline often stems from the smallest things, including being on time for meetings and sticking to agreed training sessions. The rest of the backs arrived eventually and we did get through our

Brian Moore and Ben Clarke get a dramatic view of King's Park in our helicopter ride over Durban

kicking, which improves all the time. The most encouraging thing is that the rest of the backs are beginning to enjoy the kicking exercise. An element of competition is emerging, which makes them even more focused when carrying out the drills. We all like to be winners.

Jack called the team meeting at 6.30pm before training and now it was time to concentrate on Western Samoa. One of the major factors of a World Cup competition is playing three Pool games in a week, having to change the mental focus every two or three days onto another team when normally you have a week, if not two, to slowly build-up to an international. The Western Samoans had shown in the last World Cup that they were now a major force in world rugby. They had won their two opening games against Italy and Argentina, being one of the most enterprising sides in this competition with some very exciting runners. We had them watched again in training and had studied their weaknesses and strengths on the video. It was clear that they would attempt to play the game at real pace to try and upset the rhythm of our side. English rugby is not blessed with pace and speed, whereas we have already seen in this World Cup, on the hard grounds of South Africa, that the game and reactions of other sides are particularly sharp. The Samoans are not the strongest in the set piece of scrummage and line-out, but they more than make up for it in their quick reactions around the field, including short line-outs, quick drop-outs, quick throw-ins and generally keeping the ball alive as much as possible. They also love to counter attack and any loose kicks against Western Samoa will obviously be severely punished.

Jack announced a team with many changes from the Argentina and Italy games. He had obviously decided it was time to rest some of the players who had played in both games, now that we had qualified for the quarter-finals. We considered this to be sound management which would help morale by giving as many games as possible to the full squad. Only The Judge Damian Hopley and John Mallett, the Bath prop, were not selected and so far would be the only two not to have played in a World Cup match. This is unfortunate for them, as it will probably mean they will not feature in the 1995 tournament. All the players were warned before we left that one or two might not get a game.

I was quite pleased that I was given a rest for this match, having taken a few knocks against Italy. Although my dead leg was recovering, a rest would do no harm. Mike Catt was selected for his first international at fly-half, to partner Dewi Morris, and Will was back as captain to partner Phil de Glanville in the centre. Rory had to play his third game in a week on the left wing, Ian Hunter replaced Tony Underwood and JC was recalled at full-back and given the kicking duties. In the forwards, Graham Rowntree continued at loosehead with Dawsey getting a game at hooker and Victor Ubogu back fighting for his life at tighthead where a big game would be required. Johners had to play again in the second row, and Richard West, the 6ft 10in Gloucester player, was making his debut. Big Deano was back to lead the forwards at No 8, having recovered from his hamstring injury, and he would be joined by his Leicester flyer in the back row, Neil Back. Steve Ojomoh returned to enable Rodders and Clarkey to have a well-earned rest. This was a strong enough side, in my opinion, capable of beating Western Samoa.

High flyers: all lined up for our helicopter trip over Durban, courtesy of the South African Air Force

Saturday, June 3rd

I was hoping this would be a relaxing day, particularly as I was not playing tomorrow evening, although I would be on the bench. Sara and I were meeting a couple of friends for lunch, Rob and Ginny Heginbotham, who had just arrived in Durban. Before being able to take it easy, I had a video session with Les Cusworth and one more training session. We had several tapes of the Italy game which I wanted to study, both from a personal and team point of view. There were a number of areas we were becoming concerned about, and this was a good opportunity to study the tapes with Les, who has a keen eye for the backs' lines of running and angles of attack.

At 8 am, before breakfast, I sat down with Les to go through one or two problems that had been highlighted on the video. There was a whole back-up team given the task of producing edited highlights of all of our games. We also have a video of the each game taken from behind the posts with an end-on view, excellent for the backs to see whether we are running across the field or creating space on the outside for the winger and full-back. In the two games so far our lines of running had not been up to scratch, not being straight or direct enough in getting over the gain line to give our forwards a target to move on to.

Often you do not realise how many mistakes you make until they are pointed out on film. The video showed that I had been drifting away from my scrum-half and my first two or three steps, on receiving the ball, were in a sideways direction, thereby taking up a lot of the space from the two centres, which gave them less room to move in but also makes it much easier for defending sides to drift across the field and push the attackers into touch. I had been aware of this happening in the past on many occasions and it is something I needed to be reminded of so that I can focus my attention on the problem when we go out to practice again. It's very similar to the individual aspects of rugby, like goalkicking. Unless I have regular sessions with Dave Alred, my old habits return and I start hooking the ball to the left. The video gave me an idea of what I needed to work on in training next week to improve the back play of the England squad, which had not yet functioned to its potential.

One of the problems is the quality of possession that the forwards are producing, and whether or not we are going forward. Sometimes the problem can be compounded by the backs themselves, although they do not like to admit it, by poor lines of running, which is often down to a lack of concentration and discipline in working hard to get into the right position in the first place. It's fair to say that this had happened with my own positioning, illustrated on the video. Even at the age of 32, and having played international rugby for 11 seasons, you are never too old or experienced to realise you are doing things wrong. Often the cause of the problem is an element of laziness which has crept into your game without realising it is happening. So, suitably chastened by the video camera, I was able to join the rest of the team for breakfast, having felt the last hour had been well spent.

Will was determined that today's training session would be very much like a Five Nations run-out the day before a game - short, sharp, to the point and very much a team session rather than individual units doing their own thing. Bearing in mind the number of changes to the team to play Western Samoa, and the inexperience in one or too areas, the session was a very sharp one, full of bounce and incisive running and, above all, concentration, which allowed the skill factor to be high. The session finished with a buzz we had only previously produced on two or three occasions in the two weeks we had been together.

Although it could be argued this was an inexperienced side, it was one which had been picked to win, as Jack had pointed out on several occasions. The Samoans were also missing one or two of their leading players, who were being rested or were injured, but we were confident this was a team capable of playing well, with too much fire power for the Samoans. It was important to win this game to keep the English chariot rolling, but, more importantly, it would give us a quarter-final place in Cape Town at sea level, probably against Australia. I'm not sure we really wanted to be playing South Africa in Johannesburg next Saturday, with only five days preparation at altitude for such a big game, especially as the Springboks were looking in such good form.

There had been talk of England throwing this game so we could play South Africa in the quarter-finals, and certainly the media and some of our supporters were questioning the team we had selected for the game against Western Samoa. Many thought it better to play the full-strength side that would be selected to play in the quarter-final the following week. I did not believe that was the right way to go as it was important to rest players who had played two games and also help squad morale by playing as many of the players as possible. There was never any thought or discussion of throwing an international, and nor would I ever expect there to be. We all believed this team would beat Western Samoa. Afterwards I did another kicking session with Dave and was pleased with 25 successes out of 33 kicks. Dave has kept the statistics of all the sessions we have done for both the 33 and 24 circuits. One day they will make interesting reading and he certainly refers to them to compare the build-ups to major games.

After training I met Sara at her hotel to join up with Rob and Ginny for lunch. Rob and I were at St John's College, Cambridge, together where we roomed in the second year. Rob is a full of life, loosehead prop who got his Cambridge Blue in 1984 when we defeated Oxford 34-6 with a back line that included future internationals Kevin Simms, Fran Clough, Mark Bailey and one Gavin Hastings from Scotland. Rob now plays for Henley, and is also a director of Tie Rack for whom I have been doing some World Cup promotions. I have appeared in some newspaper adverts for the company, which had unfortunately come to the attention of the tour party, and I was receiving a considerable amount of stick.

Rob had been in South Africa for a few days but Ginny, his American-born wife, arrived only this morning. It was probably one of the few times we would get to see them and we enjoyed a long and relaxing lunch at Langoustines, the famous Durban seafood restaurant. Rob is Godfather to Emily and it was a nice opportunity for him to spend some time with her as we did not see as much of our friends as we would like in London. Is there anything better than sitting in a good restaurant overlooking the waves crashing onto the beach with a clear blue sky above, the sun beating down and the Durban skyline a few kilometres in the distance, while catching up with good friends and drinking a glass or two of best South African white? Only one glass for me, however, just in case I'm required tomorrow evening. This particular lunchtime reminded me of Sydney or Brisbane where a sports freak, like myself, can enjoy an extremely attractive way of life. Even Emily and Beth seem to realise how lucky we are to be sat here in the middle of our World Cup campaign. It was like having one of those long, leisurely, time-is-of-no-important lunches the French are so famous for, briefly experienced in our year in Toulouse, and we were the last to leave the restaurant at 4pm. Sometimes these visits abroad make you question your quality of life in the UK, particularly in London.

We bid au revoir to Rob and Ginny and hoped to see them on the beach tomorrow. After a walk along the beach, we returned to Sara's hotel to watch the first half of the long awaited France-Scotland game in Pool D, which would decide who would face New Zealand, or

A swimming lesson for Emily.

the winners of the Wales-Ireland match. Who could forget the last-minute try and conversion by Gavin Hastings in Paris earlier this year in Five Nations championship, earning Scotland their first victory ever at the Parc des Princes. Would they be able to do it again, or would France get their revenge? Scotland· had deservedly taken a 13-3 half-time lead, following a mistake by Jean Luc Sadourny, the French full-back just on half-time. France had not been playing at all well, as had been the case in their two earlier games.

On returning to the England hotel, I joined several of my England colleagues in the team room to watch the second half. This followed the pattern of the first half, with Scotland tenaciously holding onto their lead and France not making any headway, apart from the kicking of Thierry Lacroix, who was to kick five penalties. With three minutes to go Scotland were leading 19-12 with a converted try not being sufficient for France, who could not afford to draw this match as Scotland had the advantage, having scored more tries in their Pool games. Therefore, when France elected to kick a penalty to make it 19-15 they were still in the hunt to score a late try to snatch victory. With Australia, they are one of only two teams in the world who have the ability to rescue an almost impossible situation. They had done this a year before with a last-minute try in the second test against New Zealand to clinch a 2-0 series victory. Here again, virtually on the final whistle and the game seemingly lost, Emile Ntamack, an ex-colleague of mine from Toulouse, went over in the corner to make the score 20-19 to France. To rub salt into the wound, Thierry Lacroix converted from the touchline and Scotland were confined to play New Zealand in the quarter-finals.

It was a result the Scots did not deserve, but was met with a certain amount of glee from some sections of the England squad. There has, unfortunately, been an undercurrent of ill feeling between England and Scotland over the last few years. This can be traced back to the bad feeling on the 1989 Lions tour, the Grand Slam encounter in Murrayfield in 1990 and also the fact that the Scots turned up to the 1991 World Cup final wearing Australian scarves after we had knocked them out in the semi-final. It was to be a miserable weekend for Gavin Hastings, as the next day he also lost his world individual points scoring record in one international (44 against the Ivory Coast) when Simon Culhane, in his debut for the All Blacks, scored 45 points in the 145-17 humiliation of Japan when he kicked 19 out of 20 conversions and also scored a try, a quite phenomenal achievement. I never thought Gavin's 44 points would ever be beaten.

The evening meeting was short and to the point and everybody knew what had to be done against the Samoans. It was down to the forwards to take control of the ball and prevent them running loose. The feeling was good among the boys and it seemed as if we were just beginning to fire on all cylinders in World Cup 1995.

England v Western Samoa

Match day today - but a rather unusual one for me for two reasons. Firstly, I was not playing, although I am on the bench; secondly, the kick-off is not until 8pm. We have become used in this tournament to moving back kick-off time to 5pm, but this would be a very long day. Rugby players are very much creatures of habit and any change that throws them out of their routine can have an impact on their performance on the pitch. We certainly found this against Argentina. To create as normal a day as possible, meetings for the backs and forwards were to be held early afternoon, while the kickers had decided to go to the ground at midday.

Rather than spend too much time in bed, which makes me feel lethargic, I wandered down to the beach at 10am. The normal problem at home is lack of sleep with work and young family commitments, but by now most of us had caught up on our sleep. I was able to spend a couple of hours with the children to give Sara a break, and also to let her father Michael have some time to himself as he had spent most of his holiday chaperoning Emily while Mummy looked after Beth. It all sounds very glamourous, popping down to the beach on a Sunday morning before a World Cup qualifying match, and there had been some pictures taken earlier in the week of Emily and I playing on the beach. One photograph in the newspapers back home tends to give the impression that this is all that the England squad are doing and perhaps we're spending too much time on the beach enjoying ourselves. I can assure you this is certainly not the case. We are all very serious about the rugby in hand. But I have to say, it is slightly unreal being based in a city like Durban with your hotel on the beachfront and the weather being conducive to wandering along the promenade and even dipping in and out of the surf. The teams based in Pretoria and Johannesburg will be finding life much more businesslike, in the fashion they are accustomed to back home. Certainly in the UK, we don't prepare for a big rugby match by playing in the sand on the morning of a game. When we move up to Johannesburg next week the surroundings will assist the squad to focus on our task in hand. It's a poor excuse to blame our Durban location, but there is a holiday atmosphere created by the behaviour of the locals and our supporters in town. Two of the most popular meeting places, Joe Kool's and Cattlemans, are within 100 yards of the hotel and everybody seems to be enjoying themselves. I'm not complaining, but it's not quite the same as preparing for a Five Nations game in January in the cold and wet of Cardiff, Dublin or Edinburgh.

However, with the whole day to fill, it was nice to be able to spend a couple of hours relaxing on the beach before switching back to game mode. This would also be the last occasion I could spend any time with the family as we move on to Johannesburg tomorrow and Sara and the children return to the UK on Tuesday. Ginny met us on the beach, but Rob had to run some errands this morning, and Emily once again had a wonderful time adding more shells to her collection and jumping up and down on the sandcastles which Daddy had patiently built. Even if the week had been a little stressful for Sara, I am sure Emily has thoroughly enjoyed herself and is looking forward to going back to school to tell all her friends about what she had been up to in half-term.

A quick jog to the hotel and it was back to the serious rugby with our regular trip down to

King's Park for myself, Mike Catt and Jonathan Callard, with Dave Alred to keep an eye on us. We had all got into this routine, and although I was not starting the game, I was still going through the same preparations as if I was playing because, as always in rugby, I could be on in the first minute. The chances of getting on from the bench against Western Samoa is always higher than against most sides due to the ferocity of their tackling, as the South Africans had found to their cost. This had some influence on the selection of today's side as we did not want to lose four or five regular players who would be required fully-fit for our quarter-final game in only six days against Australia or South Africa. Will called a backs' meeting for two o'clock as the forwards were doing some line-out practice on the car park roof. Our meeting was fairly relaxed with Will outlining what he expected from us and again emphasising the need to go out and enjoy the game.

I spent the rest of the afternoon watching a few more of the World Cup games. New Zealand had comfortably booked their passage into the knock-out games with their thrashing of Japan, while the big game today was Wales v Ireland to see who qualified as runners-up to New Zealand and a place against France in the quarter-finals. They both knew this would be the crunch game with the loser going home.

Of all the Five Nations sides, Ireland probably had the best record against Wales in the last ten years, but could they continue this at altitude in Johannesburg? They had put up the more spirited of the two performances against the All Blacks, and the Irish, on their day, can be a difficult side to combat. Strength and greater fitness has allowed England in the past decade to have a successful record against the Irish. Anything short of 100 per cent commitment against them will find you lacking. My money was on the Irish to send a sad Wales back to the UK, having failed to qualify for the knock-out stage for the second World Cup in succession. The game was virtually settled in the first ten minutes when Ireland scored 14 points with two converted tries, the first one by my clubmate Nick Popplewell from a line-out, the second from a run by the openside flanker Dennis McBride from all of 40 yards, again from a line-out and a result of some poor tackling by the Welsh midfield backs. To give Ireland such an early lead is a recipe for disaster, although the Welsh came back towards the end of a disappointing first half and improved as the second half went on. They were never able to gain the lead from Ireland and finally went down, despite scoring two tries in the last ten minutes, by the narrowest of margins, 24-23, another exciting climax.

We were hoping our game against Western Samoa would not be so close. A great deal rested on the outcome of this result - South Africa at altitude or Australia at sea level. Both had booked their passages to the knock-out stage with wins by the Aussies over Romania and the Springboks over the Canadians. The Australians had found some form in the second half against the Romanians and had run away with a comfortable 40-points victory, while the South Africans found the going tougher against a resilient Canadian side who had earlier defeated Romania by 30 points and had put up a good fight against Australia. Unfortunately, "fight" became the operative word against South Africa with a mass brawl ten minutes before the end, leaving this game and the World Cup marred by three sending offs, two Canadians, including the captain Gareth Rees, and the South African hooker, James Dalton, for fighting. The brawl was so involved that any one of half a dozen players could have gone, and it left a very bad taste after what had been, up until now, an entertaining and sporting start to this World Cup.

In the middle of the fracas was the Irish referee, David McHugh, who was left with no alternative but to send the players from the field. These were scenes that no one in the world of rugby wants to see. Although rugby is physical contact sport, and occasionally the odd punch is thrown which no one condones, the mass brawl does neither the players or the game credit. I, along with the majority of world players, are happy to see the referees and administrators take a very strong line on foul and violent play, which has no part in our game. Yes, there is intimidation, both verbal and physical, on the rugby pitch, all part of the intensity and enjoyment of the game, but when people risk serious injury from kicking and punching, as happened in this brawl, then this demands serious action. How can we possibly encourage parents around the world to let their children play our game if there are too many incidents such as this? Fortunately, strong action was taken by the officials and the World Cup administrators who were later to cite two more players by taking action on what they had seen on video evidence. I am a strong supporter of this action. I certainly don't play the game to end up in a mass brawl. Apart from one or two idiots around the world, this is the feeling of the majority of leading players. Anyone who does not share this view should not be playing the game. To the credit of administrators and referees, the game is much cleaner and safer than it ever has been. Much of this is due to the increased publicity and profile the game carries, with TV coverage allowing the administrators to act on incidents which may have been missed by the referees. The referees now also have the assistance of international officials running the touchlines who are empowered to report on foul play and can, in fact, instigate the sending off of a player. I welcome this. With everything that goes on in rugby, three pairs of eyes are certainly better than one.

It was a very pleasant evening when we arrived at King's Park an hour before kick-off. I went out onto the field with several of the backs to warm up and do some kicking drills as I would if I was playing. The crowd seemed bigger with far more England supporters. We had certainly noticed during the week that more seemed to be arriving for this weekend before moving onto Cape Town where they thought England would be playing our quarter-final. If we have to play in Johannesburg, there will be a lot of unhappy people with no way of getting from Cape Town to Johannesburg to watch us play. We needed a good start against the Samoans to put out their fire, settle our team down and get our supporters behind us. And this is exactly what we got with a try scored by Neil Back from a line-out which turned into a rolling maul, orchestrated by our own man mountain, Dean Richards, whose name was being chanted around King's Park as if we were playing at Welford Road, Leicester. Welford Road and Twickenham are not the only grounds where "Deano, Deano" rings out. We have been joined this evening by the regular band of England travelling supporters, otherwise known as the "Barmy Army", who were founded in Australia last winter while following our cricketers. Providing they don't get associated with some of the antics of our renowned travelling footballer supporters, we are more than happy to have their vociferous support. A second, well-worked try by Rory Underwood on the left-wing gave them even more to shout about, and at half-time we were comfortably ahead, having played the best 40 minutes of rugby so far on tour.

Unfortunately, our now regular lapses in concentration early in the second half brought the Samoans back into the game, with the gap being reduced at one stage to 24-17, and they were beginning to look dangerous. There is nothing worse than a Samoan rugby side beginning to hit its stride, and one or two thoughts passed through our minds on the bench of having to play South Africa in Johannesburg rather than Australia in Cape Town. However, the boys managed to hold their game together extremely well and were comforted by the award of a penalty try and also a second Rory Underwood special on the left-wing before running out 44-22 winners.

I found myself isolated on the bench at one point, being the only one of six replacements left sitting there while all my colleagues were on the pitch. John Mallett had replaced Graham Rowntree early in the second half to win his first international cap, and Tim Rodber had been called on to replace Neil Back, who had hamstring trouble. In the space of three minutes towards the end of the match, Brian Moore replaced Dean Richards, who had slightly sprained his neck and was also looking after his hamstring injury, while Damian Hopley won his first cap in place of a retiring Will Carling, who was having further problems with his troublesome ankle. Just as we had used all of our four replacements, and the place was looking like a battlefield, Tim Rodber received a cut to the head which required stitching and Kyran Bracken lost the toss with yours truly to be our fifth replacement as blindside flanker. Kyran was allowed on as a temporary replacement while Tim was stitched up. I did not fancy blindside flanker too much against the Samoans and thought Kyran's youthful enthusiasm would be far more beneficial to the team. Fortunately, we had wrapped up the game at this stage, so there was not too much panic among the replacements. I watched

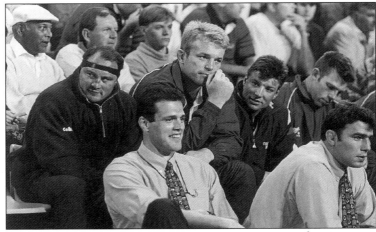

On the bench for the Western Samoan game – and I stayed there!

alone as we were guaranteed our showdown with Australia next week.

It was an uplifting performance by the team, exactly what we needed after two sub-standard performances and the huge challenge awaiting us. All the squad had now played and even the two replacements who were uncapped managed to get on the field to win their much deserved first caps for England. All those who played deserve great credit for providing just the fillip we need. The Samoans were disappointed in losing their first full international against England, which had now set them up for a very difficult quarter-final against South Africa in Johannesburg. This evening we were happy to have won three out of three and to take our chance against Australia. Perhaps South Africa, on their own soil at altitude, with only four days preparation, would be a tougher assignment.

Pat Lam, the Samoan captain for the evening, wished us well for the quarter-final clash against Australia, and he was looking forward to coming to England later in the year when we had an international at Twickenham. He also told the story of their replacement fly-half who came on just before half-time. He was told by the coach to make his tackles and "get ferocious". The young replacement had a good second-half, having a hand in one try and scoring another, and had made some very good tackles. When the game was finished, he was sat in the dressing room looking puzzled when the coach came over and said "What's wrong?" He replied: "Coach, what number was Ferocious?" It was a lighthearted note to a very successful day for England, and one which was celebrated long into the evening, especially by our three new caps - Richard West, Damian Hopley and John Mallett.

Bloodied but not beaten - Steve Ojomoh after the Argentinian battle.

Monday, June 5th

There was a buzz about the squad this morning. We had completed our Pool matches and were on the way to a massive quarter-final encounter with Australia. Although we had not played as well as we would have liked, we had certainly improved in each of the three matches, and everyone thought we were on course to put in a big performance next Sunday in Cape Town.

Before going off to the gym this morning for our usual post-match recovery training, we had to vacate our rooms and have everything down in reception by 9am to be sent off to the airport for forwarding to Johannesburg. One of the golden rules on any rugby tour, especially if you have a game the previous night, is to make sure you get packed the day before so you are not faced with last-minute rushing around when you are not feeling your best after a night of celebration. Fortunately, last night had not been too heavy for the majority of the squad, although some of the younger guys who had been awarded their first England caps yesterday were looking worse for wear.

Another hour at the gym and my swimming is definitely improving, and I also managed 20 minutes on the bicycle this morning, having not played last night and not suffering from the bangs and bruises I usually get in an international match, especially against Western Samoa. The casualty department was rather lengthy this morning with more than the usual number of players wallowing in the kiddies' paddling pool instead of putting in some earnest training. There were clear doubts about Wiggy and Backy following their injuries which forced them to leave the field. Wiggy had a calf strain and Backy had slightly pulled a hamstring. Both injuries needed a couple of days to settle down before a decision could be taken about long-term replacements if they were unable to take any further part in the tournament. It would be a blow from both a playing and morale point of view to lose any player at this stage, but it was possible that both or either of them might need to be replaced. Others who had picked up knocks included Deano, who fortunately did not appear to be too serious. It was a great relief that his hamstring had escaped any further damage, and his neck did not appear to be too bad. Tim Rodber was fine after a few stitches in his head, and Will's ankle, although sore, had not sustained any further lasting damage. Rory was still struggling with his back and shoulder, and Dewi Morris, after another outstanding performance in the thick of things, had picked up knocks to most parts of his body. He was certainly making the most of relaxing in the paddling pool whilst the rest of us were made to sweat by our fitness advisor Rex Hazeldene, assisted by Dave Alred in the swimming pool. Jason Leonard and Jerry Guscott were in their now familiar position on the cycling machines, watching the aerobic videos being played not too far away.

After a quick cup of coffee and signing a few autographs for the staff, we had lunch at the hotel before catching the 2.15 flight to Johannesburg. I had chance for one last lunch with the family which we shared with Mark and Sara Rigby, two friends from home who had spent two weeks in South Africa but were leaving shortly. I could sense that my Sara was about ready herself to go back home. We had a most enjoyable stay in Durban. We had been successful in our three Pool games at King's Park, which we all anticipated, and ended up winners of our group. I was not too unhappy, however, to be leaving Durban for the simple reason I felt we needed some different surroundings for our build-up to the match against Australia next week. Four days in Johannesburg before going down to Cape Town for the quarter-final would be just what we needed to help us focus on what would certainly be the most important game so far. As we had experienced four years ago, there had been a huge increase in intensity of our build-up for the 1991 quarter-final in Paris against France, and I was wondering how we would react to this next game knowing defeat would reduce us to innocent bystanders and an exit from the competition. We had not been preparing the last four years to go out in the quarter-final.

On arrival in Johannesburg we settled into the Sunnyside Park Hotel, just on the edge of the central district, the well-renowned murder capital of the world! Not exactly so comforting as North Beach in Durban - but then we were not on holiday. After dinner Jack called a senior players' meeting, involving myself, Deano, Brian and Will, together with Les, to formulate our plans for the week in both training and psychological build-up to what would also be the biggest game for the management as well. We discussed a lot of technical issues and how we thought this week's training should be very specific with the focus being totally on what we needed to do to beat Australia. Some of the preparation for the three previous games had been a little too general. Having to play three different games in the week, perhaps some of the team were thinking about three different teams and three different game plans. We now had no excuses - we had one game to play next Sunday and had to find one way of winning that match. No prizes for coming second. Deano and The Pitbull were convinced that we had the fire power in the forwards to match Australia, certainly in the scrum where the Aussies were having some selection problems, particularly at loosehead prop where Dan Crowley had taken over from Tony Daley where he had played for the last four years. The line-out was a big area of strength for the Aussies with John Eales probably the best middle line-out jumper in the world. We would have to work hard on this to make sure they did not dominate this area of

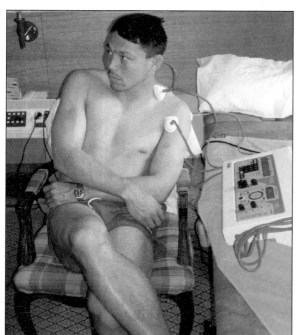

Rory receives treatment for an injured shoulder after the tough Western Samoan clash.

the game. Will and I both felt the backs had not performed particularly well so far and we needed to do some simple but specific drills to get the two centres running straight and hard at the opposition to provide a platform for our back-row forwards to get involved. If we can launch our big men running at the Australians, they would find this difficult to cope with. Although many of the Australian players had survived from the 1991 World Cup Final, the England team had changed somewhat, especially in the forwards where only Jason Leonard and Brian Moore had played in the 1991 game. The Aussies, although they had seen plenty of us on the television, had not experienced our forwards on the pitch. Much of our Southern Hemisphere rugby in the last four years had been played against New Zealand and South Africa, both of whom we had beaten. But we had not overcome Australia and this could prove to be both a positive and negative element. The Aussies would not know how strong our forwards were, but equally perhaps some of our forwards would not feel quite as confident about playing a side they had not beaten in their careers. We were sure if we were to play South Africa or New Zealand later in the competition, we were able to beat them. The knowledge gained in recent victories against these two sides would be invaluable.

We finished the meeting by informing Jack that the

Jason and Jerry enthralled by the aerobic videos.

senior players in the squad were confident that if we got our preparations right this week, both on and off the field, we had the fire power and capability to beat the Australians, notwithstanding that they were a very good side and deserved treating with respect. One or two selection issues were also discussed, in particular blindside wing-forward, right-wing and centre where there had been good performances to put pressure on the established players from Steve Ojomoh, Ian Hunter and Phil de Glanville. Victor Ubogu had also been put under pressure for his place following the switch of Jason Leonard to tighthead prop against Italy, but

he had bounced back with a much more Victor-like performance against Western Samoa and had probably done enough to guarantee his selection against the Aussies. Jack wanted to spend a bit more time thinking about the team and would announce selection tomorrow evening to give the players plenty of time to prepare. Announcing the team early would mean we could get the video analysis of the Australians out of the way at the beginning of the week so we could concentrate in the latter part on our own strengths, happy in the knowledge that we had done our homework. It was going to be one hell of a week ...

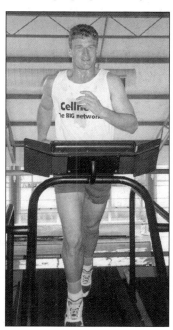

Mike Catt clocking up the miles in recovery training.

Tuesday, June 6th

The Skipper called a players' meeting before Jack's standard squad meeting at ten o'clock. Will often calls such a meeting for the players to sort out some of the problems for themselves. You have to have a great deal of trust and honesty in the squad to be successful. Out on the pitch you are on your own and there is little the management can do to help. So there are lots of occasions we like to get together and the main issue at this meeting was how we were mentally going to approach the game, bearing in mind its importance.

Rugby players are renowned for having a few beers, especially after matches. One or two have also been known to have a few before matches. In the early part of my international career, going back to the mid-1980s, it was a regular occurrence for players to drink heavily even on a Friday before an international. This had stopped in the modern game and back home there was never any alcohol consumed when we met for a Five Nations game until after the match when most players tended to make up for lost time. This had been a pretty quiet tour so far as the drinking was concerned. Really this was a necessity with three games in one week and only a couple of days to recover before another match. Will was concerned that players did not use the fact that the next match was not until Sunday as a reason to have one or two late nights. A couple of players not involved in the Western Samoa game had clearly let their hair down during the weekend and the previous evening Jack had been surprised and dismayed that this had been going on. A gentle reminder of their responsibilities and the importance of discipline, on an off the field, was needed. It's not a question of deceit, but often one or two quiet beers can lead to a four o'clock in the morning session. Will was concerned that from past experience we did not slip into this mode in the early part of this week. We had seen it happen before and had experienced going over the top as a squad, even as recently as 12 months ago in South Africa when we over-celebrated our first test win in Pretoria and found it difficult to reproduce that effort a week later in the second test. We had - we hoped - two and a half weeks of very intensive rugby left on this tour and the senior players felt it was a small sacrifice for others to make in the pursuit of excellence and success. The finger was very unfairly pointed at Jason Leonard, who likes the odd beer. Jason, in his defence, felt that one or two beers did not make any difference to him, and his excuse was that it helped him to sleep. Deano reckoned it took more than a couple of beers to knock Jason out! It was agreed, however, that we were all in this together. It would also make a victory on Sunday all the sweeter.

At the ten o'clock meeting before training Jack ran through some of the areas we discussed last night and what we planned to do in training this week. The main theme for the week was to make our game as simple as possible, get the set pieces right and have our runners being very direct, taking the ball to the Australian defence, getting across the gain line and allowing our forwards into the game. We are a much better side when we don't over-complicate things and when we are direct in our running game, chasing hard and employing our kicking strategy. In our three previous games, apart from glimpses against Western Samoa, we had not been simple enough, which helps to reduce the mistakes in the game, and is also important in keeping the pressure on the opposition. The forwards had a lot to do on producing good quality first phase ball, and the backs discussed simple ways of running at the Australians to get across the gain line, particularly at Michael Lynagh who, although a reasonable defender, we regarded as the weakest of their midfield trio of him, Jason Little and Tim Horan. Although we were not going to dwell too much on the 1991 final, when we lost 12-6 to the Australians, we did feel we were too over-complicated in this game and did not stick to our direct game plan which has proved so successful in recent years against the top sides. We are not brilliantly inventive in England, but we do have some gifted runners with the ball in hand when given space. The key at the highest level is how much space you get, and we needed to be more direct, especially from our two centres which in turn would help create more space for them, Mike Catt and the two Underwoods to exploit. It's no good being fancy in international rugby if you are playing behind the gain line because, more often than not, all you do is put your-self under more pressure and make life very easy for the defenders. Perhaps only the odd flash of brilliance from the French can contradict this statement. This time we were going to take the game to the Australians on all fronts, be very direct with a specific kicking strategy aimed at the two wingers, particularly Campese who was not only disliked but whom we felt was vulnerable under the high ball. He had also been shown in the past to be weak when it came to the physical contact side of rugby. Being brave was not one of Campo's strengths and we planned to expose this. Kicking to whoever the Australians picked at full-back - Matt Burke or Matt Pini - may not yield reward unless it was a pinpoint kick right under the posts which no full-back in the world likes (we had certainly exposed Serge Blanco in this area in the early 1990s), but we felt we could get a return by kicking to the wingers. Clearly, though, we must not kick loosely to Campo both because of his dangerous running and his own kicking abili-ty. As in all phases of play at this level, accuracy would be all important.

The other factor the players had stressed to Jack on Monday evening was the importance not to overtrain this week, bearing in the mind how much work we had already done before leaving the UK and since arriving in Durban. We did not think it was necessary to go mad. After the recovering training yesterday and the flight to Johannesburg, today was spent warm-ing up and stretching and rather than going through rugby drills we decided to have a five-a-side soccer competition to allow players to get a sweat on in a relaxed and enjoyable training session. We ended up with four teams of six due to one or two injuries and the management were drafted in to make up the numbers. I ended up with the Cornwall farmer and hooker Graham Dawe, otherwise known as the Gary Lineker of rugby following a gouging incident earlier in the season against Bristol. On being questioned about his role in this incident, Dawsey quickly responded by saying he was certainly not guilty and regarded himself to be the "Gary Lineker of rugby", a tongue-in-cheek comment if ever there was one. He was joined by The Pitbull, a Nobby Stiles-like terrier in midfield, Martin "Norman Hunter" Johnson to patrol the back and our flyer Tony Underwood to hit them on the break. The goal was guard-ed by none other than Jack "Gary Sprake" Rowell, and after two very intensely fought goal-less draws we were to face the other unbeaten side who fancied themselves as a footballing team. They were led by skipper Will Carling, Martin "The Cat" Bayfield in goal, Mike Catt, Phil de Glanville, Jeremy Guscott and their weak link, The Doc Terry Chrystal. In a bad tempered match, Brian "Eric Cantona" Moore was lucky to stay on the field following a dangerous two-footed challenge on the Skipper, who in turn was lucky not to get his marching orders for retaliation which would have left Brian booted into next week had Will made contact. Some very weak refereeing by Rex Hazeldene allowed the game to degenerate into off-the-ball inci-dents and referee abuse with very little good football. We did, however, manage to sneak two past The Cat, who was very slow at getting down to cover low shots with his 6ft 10in frame, and we carried off the England Cellnet Challenge having been unbeaten over three games. The competitive nature of the squad was already coming out and I sensed that there would be one or two more clashes before the week was out as tension mounted in the build-up to Sunday.

We had nothing planned collectively for the afternoon, although I agreed to do an interview with Sue MacGregor of Radio Four to be shown at a British Telecom conference in Birmingham the following afternoon. The sales conference was about team building and I was interviewed for ten minutes outside the front of our hotel. The aim of the interview was to have a topical subject that concentrated on team building and how we went about preparing for such a big event as next Sunday. I explained how we concentrated on the strengths and weaknesses of the opposition as well as our own strengths and weaknesses where honesty played a large part. I touched on the importance of building morale and team spirit on such a tour while giving members of the squad their own space. I was also questioned on the added responsibility of goalkicking and the effect success or failure of the goalkicker had on team morale.

After dinner we had arranged to go and see Mike And The Mechanics who were performing in Johannesburg. Some of the boys had been to see them in Durban last Saturday evening before the Western Samoan game. Apparently, all the members of the band were great England rugby fans and had even come back on stage in Durban for the encore wearing England rugby shirts. We had heard the Springbok team was also attending the concert and they promised they would keep us apart. When you are in such an intense competition as the World Cup, none of the teams want to spend much time together socially, especially with the prospect of meeting each other later in the competition. It was an excellent concert with the clock being turned back with some of the songs they played from their earlier days, including Paul Young's "Sad Cafe" era, which certainly gave his age away and reminded some of us of our school days in the late 1970s. The band was also brave enough to return again on stage with their England shirts, even in front of the Springbok team and a nationalistic Johannesburg audience, although there were a number of England supporters in the crowd who were not afraid to voice their approval - and this included the England squad. We met the band behind the scenes after the concert and although one or two were desperate for a beer to end an excellent evening, we stood around socialising and drinking Diet Coke.

Back stage in Johannesburg with Mike And The Mechanics.

Wednesday, June 7th

Although there had been a few moans about moving to Johannesburg rather than going straight to Cape Town where the quarter-final would be played, we certainly have no complaints about the standard of the hotel, although some of the rooms had to be changed initially as small, single beds for the likes of Bayf and Richard West at 6ft 10in were not exactly comfortable. But this aside, our team room facilities, and privacy therein, are very adequate. The Western Samoans are also in the same hotel and we get on very well with them. None of our supporters are in Johannesburg as they have gone straight to Cape Town, so we will not be bothered by the rugby fanatics. But a large press corps has been booked into the same hotel, hanging around the lobby and bar areas. Colin Herridge was having a difficult job trying to organise the press, so it was decided to have a daily press conference with time afterwards for one-on-one interviews. Otherwise, staying in the same hotel, they will take over our lives

Today was to see our first serious training session of the week in our countdown to Australia. The early team meeting was very specific about what we were planning to do on each of the days leading up to the game so the players were in confident mood by Sunday. This morning we concentrated on our work from line-outs, in particular the difference between forwards catching and driving line-outs and generating momentum, and spinning one or two of the loose forwards off the driving maul and into the opposition backs from which we could then attack. Also we worked on dealing with ball coming off the top of the line-out where the jumper catches and feeds immediately to the scrum-half who sets the back line moving. Off the top line-out ball gives the backs the chance to launch the midfield, particularly the two centres, across the gain line because we have 20 yards of space in which to work as the opposition backline and ourselves have to start ten yards away from the line-out. The moment the line-out ball is caught and driven, the backs can move up to just behind the maul, bringing the defence much closer to the attackers and therefore it is more difficult to get across the gain line. We felt we had to bury our line-out ploys to keep the Australians guessing and certainly our driving game was a necessary and very important part to be played by the forwards, but unless they could spin somebody off the maul and start running into the Australian midfield, it would be very little use for the backs. All we could effectively do was use it as a kicking platform to keep territorial pressure on the Aussies. Off the top line-out ball, however, could provide us with a chance to run at their midfield, in particular the Lynagh channel where we wanted to run Will or Jerry and recycle the ball quickly for either the forwards to take it on, with the back row running, or let the backs have the ball again to move wide if there was space for the wingers.

Dewi Morris had been selected in the team named yesterday following his excellent performances against Argentina and Western Samoa, which had allowed him to regain his place from Kyran Bracken. Kyran had played well against Italy last week, but Dewi's performance on Sunday had probably won him the selection. Kyran was also struggling a little with an achilles tendon problem. The management was sufficiently concerned about this injury that they called up Andy Gomarsall from the England A tour in Australia to join us as a caution in case Kyran was not fit to sit on the bench against the Australians. Andy, one of a group of very talented youngsters currently in Australia, plays for my club Wasps, although he has to fight for a first team place with Steve Bates, who was here with England on our tour last summer. Steve will be disappointed about Andy's selection as a potential replacement for the World Cup, but Jack was clearly looking to the future with one of England's brightest young players who I have no doubt will one day play at full international level. There had been no other surprises in the team and Jerry Guscott and Tony Underwood had kept their places despite the pressure from Phil de Glanville and Ian Hunter. Steve Ojomoh was also unlucky to miss out following two fine performances last week, but the calibre of our back row players is such that to break into the side with Ben Clarke, Dean Richards and Tim Rodber is extremely difficult. Victor Ubogu was back to his barnstorming best against the Samoans and we would need another big performance from him this week.

Will, Jerry and I had a discussion last night regarding the way we wanted to play. They asked me to stand a little flatter and closer to Dewi and get the ball through my hands quicker than I had in the previous games, giving them more time and space to have a go at their opposite men. We worked hard at this in training and were satisfied with the outcome. At the end of the session the forwards worked long and hard on their line-out variations and again on the scrummaging machine. As Brian pointed out on Monday night, this was a crucial area and one where he felt confident that they could match and put significant pressure on the Aussies. However, all of this only comes about following hours and hours of well thought-out and well executed practice. The forwards seem to enjoy themselves on the scrummaging machine. God knows why! But then they probably wonder why I spend so much time on my goalkicking.

Long after everyone else has departed from the training field and returned to the hotel for a quiet lunch, I was left behind with Catty, JC and Dave Alred. Today we did the 33 circuit and my mind was very concentrated during the whole of this session. It was almost as if we were actually playing the Australians and I imagined every kick to be against them. Often the problem of kicking so many attempts at goal is that concentration wavers because you don't get 33 kicks at goal in a game. However, I managed to kick 30 out of 33, my best ever return from a circuit of this nature. Let us hope that this vein continues. Catty struggled a bit today with his kicking, but as always when this happens - and it often happens to me - Dave forced him to go through with the circuit to try and tough it out mentally to get the rhythm back by the end of the session. It's an awful feeling when you can't quite get it together, mentally or physically, and you feel like chucking in the towel. It's on these occasions that you need the coach to be tough with you. The benefits of coming through a bad session and beating your own failings are enormous and Dave was pleased that Mike had managed to come back from the dead. It's difficult to explain how it all falls apart on one day and yet on the next everything seems to go perfectly. It's very hard to fight through a really bad session; those of you who play golf at whatever standard will know what I am talking about. Sometimes you want to throw away your clubs and never play the game again.

Back to the hotel for a rushed lunch followed by a compulsory outing for part-two of paint ball war games, which had finished inconclusively in Durban last week. We were taken to the outskirts of Johannesburg where this time the setting was inside a warehouse with very little room for escape apart from one door at the far end. We were all keenly anticipating this second outing, having warmed up last week. This time the guns were automatic rifles, a far more serious weapon, as opposed to the ones last week which allowed only single shots before re-cocking. I'm not sure what it tells you about the England World Cup squad when we spend our afternoons playing war games when some of the other teams go off to Sun City or on safari. The Irish, apparently, had disappeared altogether. I must try and find out from Nick Popplewell, my Wasp clubmate, what they had been up to. I wonder if they have an alcohol ban in their squad! I'm sure Jason Leonard would like to know. This was a much tougher battle between the backs and forwards. This time the forwards had been joined by Rodders, the Army expert, but he didn't seem to be too expert at paint ball as within 20 seconds he had been shot in the head by a backs' offensive, led by Flight Lieutenant Rory Underwood of the Royal Air Force. As this was a much smaller arena, we soon found the secret was to stay in touch with your colleagues so you did not become isolated and therefore risk being ambushed by half a dozen forwards with automatic rifles. Otherwise, the consequences could be very painful. I can assure you the pain can be quite significant if you are shot by a paint ball, especially if you take a direct hit to the left ear as I did this afternoon. A group of young schoolboys were also taking part and found themselves walking into a full scale battle between some of England's finest rugby players. In the end they were having great fun picking off both sides at the same time. Jeremy Thompson, from Sky News, got some great footage for our supporters back home, but his poor cameraman had to wear full headgear to protect himself from one or two stray bullets. By the end we had used up all the paint balls and the backs ran out comfortable winners as our fleetfootedness and more subtle tactics outflanked the forwards, culminating in a final ambush of The Pitbull and Neil Back. Our battle certainly helped to get the adrenalin going before our game against Australia, but Jeremy Thompson was a little surprised by the ferocity of the attacks between forwards and backs. It was decided not to have a third re-match as there was a distinct possibility that if the level of intensity increased someone would get seriously injured. I think we have probably had our fill of paint ball for this trip.

On returning to the hotel, Brian Moore called at forwards' meeting to consider the videos of their Australian counterparts. I went off with Dave to do a bit more kicking at the local ground, just an hour of punting, kick-offs and high balls. Kicking was going to be an important part of our tactics for this match and I wanted to make sure that everything was right. We got talking about training and the importance of individuals putting in more practice on their own. It's important to train as an international, once you have become one, and not, as with some players, let all the success go to your head and forget how much training you had to put in to get there. Sometimes performances lapse because of this. One player who had worked extremely hard over the last six months to win back his England place was Dewi Morris. Despite being an international who had done most things, he had worked harder than anyone to get back into the squad and his commitment and attitude in training had won him the big prize of going in against Australia on Sunday. I was delighted for him personally, having played together in most places around the world. He had even gone as far as giving up his job in December to con-

A grizzly group of forwards splattered in paint after our second war games outing.

centrate for the last six months on getting fit and working on his game for the World Cup, although he had to sit on the bench all through the Five Nations. He had been supported through thick and thin by his lovely wife Penny, as all of the girls do. I'm sure Penny and Dewi's Mum and Dad on a small farm in Crickhowel were extremely proud with what he had achieved, and I was looking forward to going into this big test him.

Thursday, June 8th

The Australian team was announced this morning and the only changes made from the side that lost to South Africa in the opening match were the replacement of full-back Matthew Pini by Mathew Burke and Tim Horan coming back into the centre in place of Daniel Herbert. Burke was a very similar player to Pini, so nothing affected our tactics.

The Australian team in full was Matthew Burke, Damian Smith and David Campese on the wings, Tim Horan and Jason Little in the centre, Michael Lynagh and George Gregan at half-back, a front row of Dan Crowley, Phil Kearns and Ewen McKenzie, a second row of Rod McCall and John Eales, and a back row of David Wilson, Tim Gavin and Willie Ofahengaue.

Today's training session was private and we were taken to a police training ground about 25 minutes from our hotel to prevent the press and opposition spies coming to watch us. There was a considerable amount of spying going on by both the media and other individuals sent by the opposing teams and it was important to find a ground where nobody could overlook what we were doing as we had specific moves planned for each of the teams. We ourselves had done our best to find out what other sides were up to in training and Austin Swain was sent on a a number of spying missions on the Aussies. The backs spent a lot of time this morning working on defence against the Australian midfield, over the years one of the sharpest midfields in the world in creating space and taking gaps. They were persisting in this competition with a lot of looping moves where Michael Lynagh would run around his inside-centre, take the ball back from his inside-centre and then hit runners either coming short or drifting wide from him, but hopefully trying to de-stable the defence by doing the loop. The South Africans showed in the opening game that this was not successful, especially as the defences in this competition were up so quickly and looping only creates complications under extreme pressure. We wanted to make sure our defensive organisation was sorted out properly, especially as looping effectively gives you an extra man in the back line by getting one player into the action twice. We had to make sure the wingers knew what was going on in defence so that they could step in early if the Australians were successful at this ploy.

Although we do not have a full set of backs against us in training, we are fortunate in having Les Cusworth as our backs' coach, in his own day no mean fly-half, to tantalise and run rings around us. The guys who are not playing in these big games make an immensely valuable contribution to our success, particularly when, as in this case, they pretend to be the Australians and work some of the moves that they are likely to come up with so we can make sure our defence is tight. It's the hardest thing in the world not to be playing and can be soul destroying for players, but we are lucky that on this trip we have players prepared to work hard for the team cause, even though they are disappointed that they are not getting many games. In particular, Phil de Glanville and Steve Ojomoh must be very disappointed they were not picked in this game after their good performances in the pool matches and, although they both know they are good enough players to be a test team, it is no consolation when time and again they are overlooked only because of the exceptional quality of the players in their position. After finishing the session I did my usual drills from the right-hand touchline, a set of 24 kicks, and also some high kicks, known as "bombs" on the stopwatch with Dave.

Following lunch I had to do my regular *Times'* article with David Hands, who was ghosting these pieces. I said that I felt we had the game plan and confidence in the team to upset the Australians and that it was not a revenge game for the 1991 final because there were only six of us in the team who lost that day and we had not played Australia since. Nine players had not had any experience laying against Australia, and in any case you don't have time to think about things like revenge in such a big game. We had enough to worry about making sure our own game plan was in order. As we had known for at least two years, time was drawing close to Sunday, June 11th which we knew was going to be D-Day in our 1995 World Cup campaign. It was clear from the intensity of our training sessions and team meetings that there was no doubt that the boys would be up for this one. It was only a question of whether we could keep the lid on our enthusiasm until the right time - which was 1pm next Sunday. It's all right being up for a game, but as with all these things timing is the key. Sometimes you have to hold things back a little bit for the game. It's no good being ready to play on Friday, and there was a slight danger that players were getting ready for this one slightly too early.

To help us take our minds off such things the social committee had decided go-karting would be a good idea for this afternoon's activity. We were whisked off to another factory on the outskirts of Johannesburg for what we thought would be a less aggressive and safer pursuit than paint ball. Teams for the one-hour endurance race were drawn up and the Dream Team of Mike Catt, Will Carling, Rory Underwood and myself looked to be the favourites from the start. Pit stops were made every five minutes to change drivers and we shot off to an

impressive early lead, due more to the incompetence of the other drivers than our own go-karting skills. However, it was clear the other teams were not going to let the Dream Team win without a fight, literally in some cases. We were being slowed down by back markers and ultimately cheating set in as our kart was deliberately rammed off the course, allowing the "Tigers of Leicester', led by Deano, to manoeuvre themselves into a winning position. The main perpetrators of the sabotage were Kyran, Ojoh and John Mallett and due to the size of Ojoh and Shep, we

The Dream Team on the starting line - but we were later punished for bad sportsmanship

decided to take it out on Kyran at the finish. The Dream Team was later punished heavily by The Judge for our bad sportsmanship.

In the evening I did a bit more kicking with Dewi and Mike to make sure we were happy with the kick-offs and punting. Mike also wanted to do some catching from high balls from Dewi and myself as we expected that he would be on the receiving end of a bombardment from Michael Lynagh, one of the best kickers in the world. Later the backs had a discussion following information gained by the Spook on one of his sorties to watch the Australians train. He had gone undetected by the Australian management, usually pretty vigilant on who was watching their sessions. But on this occasion he had managed to befriend the groundsman and his wife at the Australian training ground and had seen most of their session. It confirmed everything we had thought about their game plan, in particular the looping of Michael Lynagh and the bringing into play of Campese and the centres. After the work we had carried out in training this morning, we felt confident we could cope with this. Andy Gomarsall had also arrived this evening from Australia where he missed the England A victory over the Aussies at Ballymore. Unfortunately for Andy, Kyran Bracken's achilles problem was on the mend and Andy was surplus to requirements, but the experience of being with the England squad for the next few days would be invaluable for one so young and with such a bright future.

Mike Catt prepares for another dangerous circuit.

I also got a call this evening from my clubmate Nick Popplewell who was now down in Durban with the Irish preparing for their quarter-final match with France on Saturday. He called to wish us luck against the Australians and in typical Irish fashion said this was one of the most boring tours he had ever been on because of the intensity. Even the Irish had decided to limit their alcohol intake during the tournament. Playing international rugby at top level now demands a change in lifestyle and the days of six or seven pints the night before a game are well and truly gone.

Friday, June 9th

This is going to be one of those long, arduous days, similar to a Thursday before an away Five Nations match, when we have to travel to a new hotel in Cape Town, as well as have a training session. Rory and I had an early call as our luggage had to be down in reception by 8.30 am. Then I had to do my Radio Five interview with Eddie Mair back in London as the normal slot was impossible as we would be on our way to the airport.

Obviously the anticipation back home was starting to build up after our impressive performance against Western Samoa and people were beginning to wonder whether we could get one over on the Australians. The level of excitement was rising, and we were now down to the last two sessions before the big game. By the time we finished training today we had to know what was going on because tomorrow, under the full glaze of the world's media at Newlands, would not be the time to make any changes, or finalise any tricks we had up our sleeve. This would have to be done this morning.

The team meeting was moved forward to 9.30 to give us some extra time for training before going to the airport and again we had gone for a private session, much to the disapproval of the press looking for new angles. On the other hand, it gives them an excuse for not having to get up so early to watch us train. Some of them are clearly in need of more sleep! We again worked on our defensive pattern as a team. We also concentrated on short line-outs which we felt may be necessary against the Australians and our attacking options from these, using the big forwards not involved in the line-outs, such as Victor Ubogu, to be sent in as a battering ram in the middle of the field, hopefully sucking in the Australian defenders, allowing the backs more room for the second and third phase possession.

Our kicking strategy was worked on as an offensive weapon. In the past we have used kicking out of hand as a good attacking ploy, but there are times, unless we concentrate in training on the importance of the chasers and support runners to fill space, when we get lazy in our kick chasing, especially from the wingers and centres. We knew we would have to resort to a certain amount of kicking against the Aussies and if this was to be successful the whole team would have to be prepared to chase with an aggressive and relentless attitude. One of the ways to instill this into the players is to practice it over and over again and this puts pressure on the kickers, particularly Dewi and myself, to get the kicks in the right place. There is nothing worse than chasers being faced with a hopeless cause chasing a kick which is too long. On the big day the kicks have to be exact. We also have to organise the team defensively just in case the kicks are not to plan and the opposition are able to run the ball back at us. In particular, we need to make sure we have an effective wall across the field to eliminate the opportunities for the Australians to counter-attack from our kicks. We did not want to get into a kicking duel with Michael Lynagh and David Campese. In the past we had lost this battle because they both had prodigious length to their kicking and we did not want to find we were kicking the ball 40 yards and they were returning it, with interest, 60 or 70 yards. If Mike Catt found himself exposed at the back of our defence, we were either going to counter-attack or he would move forward and kick high balls back at the Australians to give us the chance to reorganise our defence and regain the ball. Kicking aimlessly and long to the

likes of Lynagh and Campese is a waste of time and can be very disheartening for the forwards when they see the ball sailing 60 yards into their own half.

We had to make a quick dash back to the hotel for lunch before leaving for Cape Town, so
this left very little time for kicking practice. I'm always unhappy about rushing things but there
will be plenty of time tomorrow when we train at Newlands. The England and Australian management had persuaded the World Cup Committee to allow us to fly down to Cape Town two
days before the game, rather than the day before, which had been the original plan. There
had been a lot of comment about the eight quarter-finalists having to stay in Johannesburg
until the end of the competition, or when they were knocked out, and many had requested
that they travel straight to the destination of their next game, in our case Cape Town. Provided
we could fly down two days before the game I was not too unhappy with the arrangements
as it meant we could spend nearly three weeks at altitude which will help us if we get to the
final. We discovered the Australians had sneakily travelled down yesterday, not part of the
agreement as they were staying at the same Holiday Inn occupied by the wives and girlfriends
of our squad who had moved on from Durban. The Australians had obviously tried to get one
over on us. Time and again over the years I have felt that our administrators have always had
the wool pulled over their eyes by some of our competitors who tend not to stick so closely
to tournament rules and regulations as we do. The South Hemisphere countries are always
looking to gain that vital edge which means the difference between success and failure at
international level. Our administrators have never worked in that way and, although moving
down to Cape Town one night before us was not going to have much impact on the result of
the game, it demonstrated once again the Aussies were out to do whatever they could to gain
an advantage.

As we were leaving our hotel the English press mob were desperately trying to get some of
us to make counter comments to another outburst by our beloved David Campese who had
once again started his verbal assault on the England team before another big game. Nothing
new or original in Campo's comments, but it was bread and honey to the British press, especially the tabloids. This time Campo was back on his old favourite topic of how boring
England are and that he would not pay to come and watch us. He obviously hasn't been
watching much of the rugby we have played in the last 12 months, and even if he had he
would have ignored what he saw. You can't say Campo is not consistent in his comments,
although by now the England squad were totally indifferent to them and bored stiff by his
petty whining. We had agreed at this morning's team meeting, having heard that Campo had

opened his big mouth again, that we were going to ignore his
comments and not inflame such a tedious situation. The
English press were very disappointed as we all trooped onto
the coach, every single one of us tight lipped. Nobody was
prepared to give them a quote, not that they ever needed
one to write their stories. In this instance we thought we
would let Campo do the talking and we would let our
actions on the field speak for themselves.

We arrived in Cape Town to find it had been wet and
windy as expected and the pitch on Saturday would certainly be a lot softer than we had been used to. We settled comfortably into our fourth Holiday Inn of the tournament but
the team room was unfortunately decked out in gold and
green banners as it had been the base for the Australians
during their Pool games. This immediately reminded us of
the job in hand on Sunday and was like a red rag to our
Pitbull. I don't think we will be short on determination on
Sunday.

*David Campese - the biggest
mouth in rugby.*

Saturday, June 10th

We awoke to grey skies and drizling rain at the Holiday Inn which overlooks the Newlands sports complex, the home and offices of South African rugby and the Newlands test cricket ground. We had a brief meeting with Jack before going training which, as is the norm, will be supervised today by the captain. We were allowed a very brief run on the pitch, which is all we really wanted. Most of us had been here last year for the second test against South Africa and it did not hold very pleasant memories following our 27-9 defeat, but at least we were familiar with the surroundings.

It was a very short session and we were comfortable with our game plan for the Australians. The forwards stayed for a few line-out drills and as usual I was left behind to do my goal-kicking routine. I wanted to get used to the feel of the stadium, especially as it was much softer under foot and there was quite a swirling wind. The Australians were due to arrive at 1pm for a short run-out, so we got on with a circuit of 33 kicks, split between both ends because of the wind. The ground was much softer than we had been used to up at altitude, where in winter it seldom rains and the pitches are very firm. The problem for goalkickers is that the non-kicking foot, in my case the left foot, can move by up to two or three inches which can have a significance on the contact made on the ball. Together with the wind, it was taking a while to adjust to these conditions, although they are similar to those in England. We decided it might be a good idea to put a set of extra long studs into the left boot tomorrow and planned to try this out at another session before the game. I finished with a few drop-goals at each end of the ground; you never know when these might come in useful, especially in big games which are likely to be close to the very end. I had not done much drop-goal practice and now we were at the knock-out stages it was time to put some more effort into this. At the end of the session we had a quiet word with the groundsman and he said we could come back at 8.30 tomorrow morning for our usual pre-match preparation. To keep him sweet we had to promise to bring an England polo shirt with us. The ground staff at Newlands were surprised at how much work I put in and were even more surprised that I was planning to come back before the game.

Just as we were leaving the Australian coach arrived and Campo and I exchanged glances without actually saying anything. Tim Horan, in the usual Aussie fashion, said "G'day Mate" and had a conversation with Dave Alred who had made three trips to Australia coaching their backs during our winter. They were disappointed he had decided to join the England squad, but being from Bristol it made more sense being part of our set-up, although clearly they appreciated the quality of the work he had done for them.

The weather took a horrible turn for the worse when we arrived back at the hotel with grey, swirling low cloud enveloping Table Mountain, bringing a torrential downpour for much of the afternoon. Fortunately, we had just finished practicing and the Aussies had just started. These were conditions they would not be looking forward to tomorrow. We were not bothered either way, but were more used to playing in such terrible conditions in the UK. I did not envy them their training session in pouring rain. The afternoon was conveniently filled by watching two of the other quarter-finals - France v Ireland in Durban and later South Africa v

Western Samoa from Ellis Park in Johannesburg where the final would be held. Neither game turned out to be particularly enthralling or spectacular. Although Ireland held France 12-12 at half-time, it seemed they had run out of steam up front and were not capable of holding the French who ran out comfortable 36-12 winners. They had two late tries, one an interception, to flatter the score in their favour. We had harboured hopes that Ireland would be able to test the French, bearing in mind the way they had played against New Zealand, and also the fact that France were still stuttering in the competition. It was evident, even in the first half, that Ireland had blown up and were not able to give France too much of a test and they would be on the next plane home. The South Africans were expected to win comfortably against Western Samoa as they had beaten the Samoans 60-8 only two months earlier. There was some concern about the Samoan tackling, very physical to say the least, if not dangerous, with their speciality shoulder-high body charges. The South Africans were not relishing another battle with the Samoans. However, once again the result went as expected with South Africa winning 42-14, despite suffering a couple of serious injuries to Andre Joubert, who broke his hand, and rib injuries to Joost van der Westhuizen and Mark Andrew caused by heavy tackles. (The Samoan full-back Mike Umaga was to be cited the following day by the Rugby World Cup Committee for dangerous and late high tackles which had gone unpunished by the referee, Jim Fleming.) So the first semi-finalists were known - France against the host country South Africa, to be played next Saturday in Durban. Everything was going to plan with the seeded nations going through to the semi-final and tomorrow would be our turn against the Australians, while New Zealand take on Scotland.

For our team meeting this evening we quickly went through our game plan which had been well rehearsed in training this week. We just wanted to recap and make sure everyone was happy. We had settled on reasonably conservative tactics, based on good first phase possession which we hoped to secure from the line-out and scrum where, although John Eales was a major force, we felt we could dominate. The Australians were not the biggest scrummagers in this World Cup and we should be able to carry out backrow moves off the scrum, allowing us to get into the Australian midfield, particularly at Michael Lynagh. Having achieved the aim to get across the gain line from the set play, we then wanted to bring our big forwards into the game and allow the centres to keep running at the Australian midfield and just keep recycling the ball either until they made mistakes and gave penalties away by going offside, or until we created enough room for our wider men to run at them. Although we were all happy with the game plan, I could sense there was still an air of uncertainty around, mainly caused by the fact we had not played against the Australians for four years. Many of this team had never played against them at full test level. This is a situation that must be rectified for the good of English rugby. We can't go four years without playing against the world champions, from one World Cup to the next. There is really very little you can do about the fear of the unknown. We had learned so much about the quality of our own team and the confidence we had gained from victories over New Zealand and South Africa in the last 18 months, but there is no substitute for playing against a team like Australia. Having played against them so many times between 1987 and 1991, both for England and the British Lions, I was confident we had chosen the right game plan and had the players capable of upsetting the Australians who had still not functioned well in this competition and were looking a little bit off the pace. And I certainly thought we were good enough to beat them.

At the end of the team meeting the management were asked to leave for Will to say his few words to the players on their own. The Spook was also asked to stay behind to address the squad collectively. He handed out a sheet of paper to all the players which contained the numbers one to 21 and then asked us to write one of two positive sentences on each player in tomorrow's team. This was the first time he had done anything like this with the squad and he wanted it taken seriously. Designed to build up confidence, it took about 40 minutes for everyone to write down comments on the strengths of the other players. Each number was then placed in an envelope and later in the evening Austin handed each player an envelope containing 20 statements made about you by the other players. Reading those comments later, both Rory and I, who had been around a long time, were so moved by the comments of the other players that we both said we would keep them. After dinner we finished off our social engagements which included a brief drink with Howard Ford, the Managing Director of Cellnet, our major World Cup sponsor, and Gillian MacCarthy, the Marketing Manager who looks after the England team. As Normal, Rory and I rested easily this evening ready for tomorrow's big game.

It's a hard life being a snapper.

Me and Mike Catt out on the pitch sampling the atmosphere.

England v Australia

D-Day had arrived. It never gets any easier, no matter how many games you have played at this level. But I was helped by having the routine of kicking practice on the morning of the game to pass the time, rather than just sitting around the hotel worrying about what was going to happen.

With a one o'clock kick-off, we needed to be up reasonably early and had to be at Newlands by 8.30am as dictated by the groundsman because they still had more work to do on the pitch. We went through our routine on a much drier Cape Town morning. Although it was reasonably windy, the groundsman anticipated that by one o'clock they weather would have cleared for a dry afternoon. The morning of a matchday is always difficult to fill in, that's why the kicking is always important to relax me and get me away from the pressures of the hotel where other players are lounging around, taking a long breakfast and not saying very much. We did our usual pre-match preparation, a bit of punting and a few kicks at goal along the try-line to hit the posts. This afternoon it is very likely that kicks will decide the game. The backs met at ten o'clock while the forwards were in the car park as usual going through a few line-out throws. As with the meeting yesterday, most of the talk from Will was very positive. It was important we got off to a good start with the backs making a real effort to help the forwards get going with kicking, chasing and driving across the gain line - backs supporting backs as we had been working so hard on in training during the past weeks.

I managed to get a quick call into Sara to see how she was feeling at home. In these situations she is always far more nervous than I am, especially being so far from the action. Her mother Diana was coming over to help look after Emily and Beth to give Sara the chance to watch the game in reasonable peace, although I could tell she was not really looking forward to it.

When we arrived at Newlands we were encouraged by the huge number of England supporters who were in Cape Town. We had been told to expect somewhere near 10,000 England supporters for this weekend and it really does make a difference having so many cheering you on so many miles from home. The dressing room before such a big game is generally very quiet as players are concentrating on their own job. It is important to relax some players by getting them talking so they do not actually freeze. Several of the backs - Mike Catt, Jonathan Callard, myself and usually Jerry Guscott - like to get out onto the pitch for 20 minutes, kicking and generally getting used to the atmosphere and playing conditions. I like to get out of the dressing room rather than spend up to an hour and a quarter in such a claustrophobic atmosphere. As a final check I do one or two goal kicks down the try line and I've got into the habit of having to hit the post to feel good. We had to go out onto the pitch six minutes before the kick-off, time for television to screen the anthems and get in a few more advertisements. In this competition they have asked both teams to run out together, which does not happen back home for the Five Nations. This is something we don't like as we prefer to go out as separate entities and hear the applause of our own supporters.

When we ran out for the start of the game it was like playing at Twickenham and we felt we had a lot of the neutral South African support keen to see us beat the Australians. There were not too many Australians in the stadium and the crowd advantage that we had could be crucial by the end of the day. The Barmy Army had started their campaign in Durban last Sunday and had moved on in force to Cape Town, supplemented by other fanatics who had arrived this week. We were filled with pride and passion as we sang the National Anthem to an almost packed Newlands, and one which seemed to have 80 per cent England supporters.

The first 25 minutes of the game was probably the best periods of play we have put together for some time, certainly eclipsing anything else in this World Cup, and possibly matching the first 20 minutes against South Africa in the first test last summer. In this period we managed to score 13 points, which gave the boys up front an awful lot of confidence against a side they had not played against before. We were really taking the game to the Australians. Their confidence was knocked again as it was in their first game against South Africa. Apart from our own attacking game, we were putting the Aussies under huge pressure in midfield and their looping tactics became their undoing when Michael Lynagh dropped the ball in a loop with Tim Horan just outside our 22. I was able to pick the ball up quickly and feed to Jerry Guscott, who came up on my right shoulder. He fed Will Carling, who put Tony Underwood away for a 60-yard run down the righthand touchline before just escaping the clutches of Damian Smith on the far Australian tryline, rounding him and planting the ball jubilantly for our opening try. At this point we were 13-3 up against the world champions and dominating in almost every phase of the game. What a dream start! But within two minutes of either side of half-time our lead had been eclipsed, firstly by a penalty from Lynagh just before the break, and secondly almost from the kick-off when the Australians were awarded a scrum. Lynagh put up a pinpoint high kick to our righthand corner where Tony Underwood and Mike Catt could not outjump Damian Smith, who ran a perfectly timed leap and catch to come down over the tryline. The Aussies are the best in the world at this. Time and again we have seen Tim Horan and Jason Little chase high kicks, catch them on the fall and score tries. A touchline conversion from Michael Lynagh had brought the scores back to 13 all. Psychologically, this was not a great thing to happen to the England team so soon after half-time.

We were pumped up for a big second half, believing there were certain areas we could improve on. As Brian Moore quietly pointed out to the Skipper at half-time, one of them was not to get into a bloody kicking contest with David Campese, a reference to Will having punted the ball twice to Campese's wing who in turn had returned the ball 60 yards down the touchline, putting us back under pressure in our own half. Will was the first to hold up his hand and apologise. Brian obviously wanted to get this off his chest and Will asked him to concentrate on what the forwards were going to do better in the second half to keep the pressure on the Australians and not let this lead slip. Within one minute we had done just that and it reminded me of Will's half-time talk in the quarter-final in 1991 in Paris when we were leading 10-6. He finished by saying the next team to score would probably win this match. Unfortunately for Will, within about five minutes the French had scored a try in the corner by Jean-Baptiste Lafond to level the scores and as we were stood under the post waiting for the conversion, Mike Teague, in his laconic Gloucestershire accent, took one glance at Will and said: "Now what are you going to say." On each occasion, however, we managed to battle through and come out as victors.

The second half against Australia, however, was probably mentally the toughest 40 minutes of international rugby I have ever had to play. It was not the most scintillating rugby to watch in terms of quality, but purely because of the closeness of the score and the lead changing hands throughout the whole of the half. I am sure it kept the spectators both here and at home on the edge of their seats and there was a noticeable change in the noise coming from our supporters as we battled it out with the Aussies in the second half. They were so concerned and nervous they found it difficult to say anything. England went 16-13 up only to be levelled and then we found ourselves 19-16 down to level 19 all. Then we went 22-19 down about 15 minutes from the end of the game. With only six minutes left and still trailing by three points, many in the crowd and at home thought our chances were slipping away. When you are out on the pitch and you can see the clock ticking away, a part of you thinks this is not going to be your day, but you know, having been in situations like this before, you never give up. You keep trying to play your game. Neither side had achieved any ascendancy in the second half and it was a nervy, cat and mouse affair. We were the wrong side of the scoreboard when we were awarded a penalty which, if kicked, would draw us level with exactly five minutes left to play. It was not a particularly difficult kick as far as I was concerned, being 25 metres out and 15 metres in from touch on the left, but it was certainly the most difficult mentally I have ever had to take. Five minutes to go, World Cup quarter-final, knowing that if this was missed we would be out of the competition. This was when all the hours of practice and technical expertise that Dave had passed on was going to prove its worth. This is when you have to know your technique is good enough to see you through. I have never been so relieved to see a kick heading in the right direction, the touch judge flags flying. We were still in the game and would settle for extra time. One or two situations still developed which could have seen us out of the competition. First of all, the Australians had a scrum on our 22 from which I felt sure Michael Lynagh would attempt a drop goal. The Aussies even did a backrow move first to try and pull in some of our loose forward defenders to give Michael more time, but our defence managed to snuff out their attack. A drop goal then, with only minutes left, would have been a deadly blow. He had shown in the quarter-final against Ireland in 1991, when he had a similar position to drop a goal to draw the match after Ireland had taken a dramatic lead in the last few minutes, that he would go for the try and in fact scored himself in the corner. Again he obviously thought they were good enough to score a try, but they had not really penetrated our defence all day, so I was very surprised he did not attempt it. Even then we did not completely clear our own 22 and even the mercurial David Campese tried a drop goal from a relatively easy position, but fortunately for us he skewed his kick well wide. After all Campo's criticism of England's style, and particularly my kicking, how ironic it would have been if a drop goal from him had won them the game. I'm sure the media and Campo himself would not have been so critical of such kicking tactics had that been the case.

We were all expecting the final whistle when we were awarded a penalty just outside our own 22. I handed the ball to Mike Catt to find touch as Catty had been striking the ball really well out of hand in this game and when doing so he kicks the ball five or ten yards further than I do. All we needed was for Mike to find touch to give us the line-out throw-in. The last thing we wanted was a mistouch with Australia having an opportunity to counter-attack. He did this fantastically well and drove the Aussies into their own half. On the way to the line-out Martin Johnson turned to me and said: "What do you need for a drop goal." My response to both him and Dean Richards, who was also thinking along similar lines, was: "I need it to be caught and driven a few yards to pull in the Australian backrow and then delivered as the drive is still going forward." All we needed now was the perfect throw from Brian Moore, the perfect catch from Martin Bayfield, the perfect drive by the rest of the forwards in field to take me closer to the posts and a simple drop goal and we would be in the semi-final of the World Cup. If only is it was this easy, I thought as we ran towards the line-out. The first parts of the exercise were carried out with military precision as Brian found Martin Bayfield in the middle of the line-out and he took a clean, two-handed catch high above John Eales who had caused Bayf a lot of problems in the second half. The forwards then drove on and in field and Dewi fired the ball out to me. In these situations you have to revert to automatic pilot and you don't really have time to think about the consequences of your actions. As with the goalkick five minutes earlier, my main concern was with technique, particularly keeping my head down. The rest was in the lap of the gods but I knew as soon as I had hit it that it would certainly have the distance, despite being 40 yards out, and it was only a question of direction. I eventually raised my head and saw it heading towards the righthand post as there was a slight breeze taking it in that direction. Jerry Guscott was the first to react, clearly being more confident than I was that it was going over. In a split second I too realised that the wind wasn't going to spoil our day by which time Jerry and I were doing virtual cartwheels on the way back to the halfway line as the rest of our colleagues were still watching in disbelief as the ball sailed high between the posts.

I don't think I can honestly remember having hit a drop goal quite so cleanly from so far out and having it still going up as it sailed through the posts. It was an incredible sight. The feeling of real joy and excitement as it does go over cannot really be contained and this was why I was running back at this point punching the air. For a split second I forgot exactly where I was. I'm sure back home there were few living rooms erupting with screams of laughter and joy. We hardly had time to enjoy it when the Australians had taken a quick kick-off, going the wrong way to try and catch us unawares. One or two of our boys were still celebrating as some of them thought the final whistle had gone. We had to regroup and prevent the Aussies having one last counter-attack to get themselves into our half and within drop goal or penalty range. There was as mad scramble for 90 seconds until Dewi calmly put the ball into touch near the Australian corner flag, despite the vociferous efforts of Will and myself begging him to kick into touch sideways just to get the ball off the field of play. Dewi, being the cool head he is, produced one of his best kicks of the afternoon by putting the ball over Damian Smith's head with three bounces into touch, well out of danger's way. He would not have been too popular had he mistouched and Damian Smith caught the ball and been able to counter attack. The final whistle came to put us out of our misery and there were some strange scenes in the dressing room. One or two tears were shed and it was even reported that Dennis Easby kissed Will Carling. I have to say I didn't see this but I was assured it did take place. Some of the

Dewi protects his modesty after our quarter-final victory over the Aussies.

guys on the bench had not been able to watch the last five minutes and Phil de Glanville and Steve Ojomoh spent most of this time in the tunnel, peering out only when there was a cheer to find out what had happened, such was the tension. Jack Rowell described the scenes after the game as "very emotional" on the bench and also for the wives and girlfriends who were still with us and were finishing their trip on the highest of highs. Like most of the guys on the field, I was absolutely shattered and could barely speak as I was ushered into the TV room for an immediate post-match interview with Jim Rosenthal. The tension had almost been too much and finished in such a dramatic fashion that very few of us were able to speak coherently about what had occurred as we were mentally and physically exhausted. All of us had found it really difficult in that second half, knowing that one mistake by any single player in such a tight game could cost the whole competition. The look of Dewi Morris' face as he was penalised at a scrum by David Bishop, the referee, to give Michael Lynagh the chance to put them three points ahead, said it all. Dewi was aghast at the decision. Nobody does these things on purpose, but it is very waring when you have to be so mentally tough for the whole 40 minutes.

Everybody was in a state of shock in the dressing room which was laden with bodies. We just did not have the energy to celebrate such a momentous victory. It was almost too much.

Les let me have his Cellnet mobile phone so I could immediately ring Sara, knowing she would be in a much worse state than me. And true enough, she had hardly been able to cope with the second half. She was pleased to hear from me so soon after the game and it would take her some time to calm down. I dreaded to think what my mother would be like at home, knowing how much she hates it when I have to do the kicking. We managed to pull ourselves together and regroup for the reception after the game. Michael Lynagh, the Aussie captain, was very gracious in defeat, as were all the Australians, including Campo. Although they were obviously disappointed, they hid it well and wished us all the best in our game against the All Blacks next week. I had a chat with Mark Harthill, the reserve Australian prop, with whom I had played club rugby with Gordon in Sydney back in 1986, to find that the club was going really well, having won the Australian championship two years ago, although he was the only one left from the team in which I had played. There were rumours flying around that David Campese had announced his retirement. Although not confirmed, this was greeted with derision from the England dressing room. I also had a brief word with Michael Lynagh as the Australians left the reception. I first played against him in 1983 and had a great deal of respect for such a fine player. He was unsure whether this would have been his final game for Australia. They were playing New Zealand in the Bledisloe Cup about three weeks after the World Cup final and he would be considering his future between now and then. He was obviously a shattered man, having to go back home as captain of the side that had given away the World Cup when there had been so much hype and expectation in Australia.

Before leaving the ground we managed to catch a glimpse of the other quarter-final that had kicked-off at three o'clock in Pretoria where New Zealand were taking on the Scots. From what I saw it was looking a bit one-sided and the game was virtually over just after half-time. Jonah Lomu was causing the Scots as many problems as he had caused Wales and Ireland, and he was obviously going to be a big headache for us next week. For the moment, however, we would concentrate of celebrating our great victory over Australia and we would worry about the All Blacks next week. We regrouped in the hotel team room for a quiet beer and although there was a great deal of satisfaction around, the combination of extreme tiredness plus the realisation that this was only the quarter-final resulted in the celebrations being somewhat muted. We had always set out to come here and win the World Cup but, although this was a great victory, there was a long way to go yet. On the way to dinner at the Cape Town Waterfront we had the misfortune of our coach breaking down before we arrived at the girls' hotel, which allowed Will Carling to come out with the quote used in the papers later in the

week: "Don't worry, Rob's with us so we can walk across the harbour to our restaurant." Clearly, I would be receiving some more friendly stick from the troops after what had happened this afternoon. A long and enjoyable evening was had with our supporters in the Sports Cafe where, along with hundreds of the Barmy Army, I managed to run into two college mates, Rob Heginbotham and Richard Rothwell. Heggers and Ginny I had already seen in Durban and now Ricky had turned up in Cape Town for one of those memorable days as we celebrated until the early hours.

We did it! Dressing room celebrations with Tony Underwood and Mike Catt.

Monday, June 12th

Cape Town on a Monday morning with a hangover is not the worst place to be, especially when you wake up to the knowledge that you have dumped the world champions out of the competition. Despite this, we were up reasonably early to catch our flight back to Johannesburg where we will be staying for the next week.

Before thinking about the All Blacks, we have been given the respite of a couple of days in the gambling capital of Sun City to relax after a tough few days and to let the boys recharge their batteries for what was going to be another huge mountain to climb next Sunday. The snappers were up early to catch the players at the hotel and were keen for a few shots in the car park on a sunny day with Table Mountain clearly visible in the background. One of the peculiarities of Table Mountain is that it is often cloaked in its white cloud tablecloth, but this morning it was majestic as it peered down over this beautiful city. And as far as we were concerned, everything is beautiful this morning!

Will and Dawsey relaxed by riding around the car park on one of the Police outrider's motorbikes and generally the atmosphere was very relaxed. There were a few tired and emotional goodbyes as we boarded the coach for the airport and the girls were left behind as their part of the World Cup was about to end with them leaving Cape Town this evening. The support and love they had brought with them would be missed, although we knew they would be right behind us back home.

I gave a couple of final TV interviews on the bus to the airport on how I felt the morning after such a big day for English sport, and most of the next four hours were spent asleep, two hours on the plane and a couple of hours on the coach up to Sun City. We arrived tired but happy and ready for a quiet evening, although the temptations of the casino and gambling tables were too much for most of the party to resist. The only problem with gambling is that you always end up losing. Even when you have a winning spell, you tend to go on a bit too long. If I had a pound for every time one of the boys had said "If only I had stopped a bit earlier" I would be a very rich man. Unfortunately, the craze bit a few of them badly and Rodders, Catty and Deano found that most of this week's £22 daily allowance had already been spent on the first night.

We had visited Sun City for just a day on our trip to South Africa last summer but we had not be able to see all the sights. I was looking forward to switching off totally in the next couple of days to see what Sun City really had to offer, having heard some mixed reports about its quality. Certainly there were no complaints about the Palace Hotel. We had planned to stay here just for the one night, but Dennis Easby, who had patched up his relationship quite successfully on the tour, had kindly agreed to let us stay another night with the bill picked up by the RFU. Unfortunately, their coffers did not extend to picking up some of the gambling debts. The gesture was much appreciated as these couple of days would be important in our recuperation for next weekend. The sheer scale and quality of the hotel was something to behold in stark contrast to the Holiday Inns where we had been staying. We were happy to be indulging ourselves in the luxury of this South African paradise.

Tuesday, June 13th

Rory and I thought we would be the early birds to catch the worm this morning by being up and on the first tee of the Gary Player Country Club by 9am. We were kindly provided with a couple of sets of Mizuno golf clubs by the sponsors of footwear to some of the squad. Being an Adidas man myself, I was obviously reluctant to be pictured playing with Mizuno clubs, so we decided to get off before any one else hit the course.

Our caddy Zac, who had been here since the course opened in 1979, knew exactly which clubs to play and how the greens lay. He was no mean coach for the Andrew golf swing, pretty poor at the best of times, and by the end of the round I felt a distinct improvement. We had decided not to play the Lost City golf course where last year I lost about 20 balls. This shorter and wider Gary Player course was much more suitable. If we come back to Sun City again after beating New Zealand, maybe I'll brave the Lost City again, a much more difficult course, not withstanding the crocodiles on the 13th green which had become infamous the world over. After stopping off at the Halfway House following probably my best shot of the day on the ninth when I chipped onto the water surrounded surface, Rory and I decided to make a couple of calls, rather illegally and cheekily going down the tenth following rejuvenation by a Mars bar and a cup of coffee. It was a beautiful South African winter's morning with clear blue skies and bright sunshine. And here we were on the Gary Player Country Club course, home of the million dollar classic in November, and there was hardly a single person on the course which, quite extraordinarily, we had to ourselves. I had said I would never do this, but I just had to ring John Page in the office to say I was having a tough time choosing which club to use for my approach shot to the tenth green. I'm sure this went down very badly in the office, but at least I was thinking of them. To make things worse, John and James Max had been rather busy, not least because our boss, John Rigg, had decided to come to Cape Town this week. I met him briefly with David Watt, another director of DTZ who, along with two other colleagues, had arrived to see our game against Australia on Saturday. They were both sports fans, particularly rugby, and were looking forward to a pleasant week in Cape Town on the golf course before seeing us again next Sunday. So none of us were particularly popular in the office and my call did not help things. I also rang by best man Andy "Taff" Davies to see if the Welsh team had arrived home safely following their failure to qualify for the knock-out stage, which raised his hackles. He was less impressed when I told him where I was. He only retort was: "Well, I've been round that course myself". Rory rang in to say he would be a couple of weeks late for the next flying mission and was given permission to stay on by his base commander. Reaching the semi-finals means we have two more weeks in South Africa and even if we don't make the final we have to stay on for the third and fourth place play-off in Pretoria on June 22nd. But it's the final we have got firmly in our sights.

The golf was finally finished by a very pleasant lunch in the clubhouse overlooking the Lost City course where Jack and Les were just starting their second 18-hole round, having completed the Gary Player course. We thought we would have more fun attacking the waterworld attractions in Sun City rather than another round of golf. We joined the rest of the lads doing a good impression of schoolchildren on a day's outing, lying around on the artificial beach by the wave machine, inter-mixing this with trips down the water shutes. The sight of ten international rugby players going down the water shute in ten rubber rings fastened together was not a particularly pretty one or terribly safe if you're the first one out at the bottom. For the first time in my life I ventured down one of these wretched shutes and was impressed with my bravery, particularly going through the narrow and totally dark shute with a 12 second time from top to bottom, let

Ready for the water chute in Sun City.

alone the vertical drop which even some of the seasoned loonies found a little heartstopping. I think the attendants were glad to see the back of these mad Englishmen out in the midday sun.

Before dinner Will and I had a chat in the bar with Bob Templeton, the Australian forwards' coach who had stayed on for a couple of days and with John Eales, the second rower, had followed us up to Sun City for a spot of relaxation and golf. Tempo had spent some time in England coaching Harlequins and therefore knew Will, Brian and Jason very well. He was still pretty unhappy about the Australian performance on Sunday and indeed all of their World Cup performances. He was very unhappy the way the Australian backs had played, which I have to say is often the case coming from a forwards' coach. On this occasion, he had good reason for the Aussies had continued with their looping tactics which we had identified in their game against South Africa. In fact, the crucial try scored by Tony Underwood on Sunday had come from a mistake in such circumstances. Tempo was not happy that the Aussie backs had gone against the advice given by their advisory panel which consisted of 12 former Australian inter-nationals who fed information on the opposition into the captain and coach and advised on the tactics for any one international. Clearly the Australians were very professional in the way they approached international rugby and had prepared meticulously for this tournament since 1991 with the sole intention of taking the Webb Ellis trophy back to Australia. Obviously a lot of time and money had gone into this exercise. Tempo was angry that the backs had gone against the advice not to carry on with the looping. There had been one or two problems in the Aussie camp that had not come to light, and it was obvious from their performances they were not playing to the level expected to win this World Cup. Knowing the Australians, there would be some harsh words said when they got home and some jobs on the line, particular-ly Bob Dwyer's, the coach for seven or eight seasons, even more so if New Zealand go on to win the World Cup and then beat the Australians in the Bledisloe Cup later in the year. The Aussies were therefore very keen to help us in our game against New Zealand on Sunday.

After dinner Jack called a meeting of senior players to discuss tactics and training for this week and how our game plan would differ. We had no doubt that mentally we could sort our-selves out in time and we were good enough to beat the All Blacks. If anything, most players would find this game easier to prepare for simply because many more of us had played against the New Zealanders; in fact 14 had beaten them at international level. Only Mike Catt had not played against New Zealand as an international. Nothing was going to change very much against the All Blacks as we felt our set piece possession could be well secured, although the

Set for another death-defying plunge.

All Blacks were better scrummagers than the Australians, and they were more streetwise in the art of spoiling lineout possession. We had first-hand experience of this in 1993 when, after the Lions had won the second test 20-7 in Wellington and had gone into the third test with the series at one all, we were handsomely beaten by the All Blacks who changed their forward tactics considerably to cause Martin Johnson and Martin Bayfield a lot of problems. We could expect a similar situation on Sunday. Brian and Dean thought they could cope with these problems this time around as Johnners and Bayf were far more experienced. But it was still going to be some test. Having won good first phase possession, we still wanted to attack the fly-half channel, in particular the new boy Andrew Mehrtens, already one of the New Zealand stars in this tournament. We wanted to see what he would be like under pressure. We also knew that Walter Little and Frank Bunce in the centre were very strong tacklers and our best chance of making the gain line was in the Mehrtens' area. We had proved against Australia that we were capable of getting into this channel and we felt we might be able to exploit the perceived lack of team organisation in the All Blacks' defence by spreading the ball wide to our wings. To do this, the backs would have to stand a little deeper as their centres and wings fly up very quickly from defence and need to be outmanoeuvred rather than run through. There are no harder tacklers than Frank Bunce who played for Western Samoa in the last World Cup, and heavy, front-on tackles are one of his specialities. There was no doubt that we and Jack felt we were good enough to beat this team.

Having avoided the losses in the Sun City casino last night, I felt compelled to have one trip to the Black Jack table as I couldn't possibly leave this place without having a dabble. Unlike some of our squad, I'm not one of the world's biggest gamblers and I left before too much damage was inflicted. Some of the others never know when they are beaten until it is too late by which time there's a lot of hasty borrowing going on and a desire to get back to Deano's card school which had been fleeced by Andy Gomarsall on his brief visit last weekend. He went back to England with a much healthier bank balance than when he arrived.

Wednesday, June 14th

We were just beginning to get used to our holiday retreat in Sun City but this morning we had to pack up and head back to Jo'burg to start our preparation for Sunday's big game. I was under the impression that some of the players were still mentally and physically jaded but we had plenty of time to get ready. After all, it was not as if we were starting from scratch; we have been here for several weeks and have played and won four internationals.

On leaving the Palace Hotel, I managed to have a quick chat to Mark Ella, the legendary Wallaby fly-half who scored a try in each of the Australians' grand slam of victories against England, Scotland, Ireland and Wales in 1984, the last tour of its kind. He was one of the game's most gifted runners of the ball, and the sleight of hand of the Ella brothers, Mark, Glen and Gary, is world renowned through their Randwick (Sydney) club and international days. He is now one of the advisors to the Australian Rugby Union, and he, too, was disappointed with the way they had performed in this competition. Alan Jones, the former Australian coach in the 1987 World Cup, and now a media personality in Sydney, had spoken to me just before we left home. He felt the Aussies were not properly equipped for this World Cup and that too many of them had their minds elsewhere, particularly with regard to the Super League which would be throwing so much money at the Aussie players after the competition was finished. It was rumoured that players like Jason Little had been offered a million dollars to switch codes after the World Cup. It was obvious that some of them would have problems totally focusing on the job in hand. From these discussions, it looks as if there will be a number of changes in Australian rugby after this World Cup.

The coach trip back to Jo'burg was more lively than the one up to Sun City when most players were asleep. The banter returned to the back of the coach with most of the stick, handed out by the Skipper and his parrot, Martin Bayfield, being taken by The Monkey, Dewi Morris. Jason Leonard jumped on the bandwagon, providing none of the stick came his way, and the spirits were high as we arrived back in Johannesburg.

After lunch we were back into our training routine and we went down to the famous Wanderers Rugby Club on the outskirts of the city which backs onto the Wanderers test cricket ground. This was supposed to be a private session but unfortunately the pitch was overlooked on all sides and among the spectators were several ex-Springboks, including Ian Macdonald, and current Springbok Pieter Hendriks who had been banished from the tournament for his part in the brawl against Canada. So any specialist work for the New Zealand game was out of the question. In any case, a lot of the work the forwards wanted to do this early in the week was the heavy scrummaging and mauling to get it out of their system. Forwards like to go through set routines but the backs are more flexible because of the nature of the individuals involved. While the forwards got on with their heavy contact work, we had a relaxing game of touch rugby which turned out to be very competitive. 'Touch' was not exactly the correct description of some of the contact going on. We finished with some more punting with Dave Alred, who thought it was important that we all got back into our stride after a couple of days off. We had had our little rest. Now it was time to switch on again and get back to the serious business. We were just one step away from our dream of being in the final of the 1995 World Cup. I stayed behind to get the kicking going again and got back into the groove nicely in the perfect conditions of altitude training. The ball certainly flies a lot further up here in Jo'burg. I did a routine of 40 or 50 kicks at goal to keep the leg muscles going.

This evening we started to build up our mental preparation for the Kiwis, putting the Australian victory behind us and focussing totally on the black shirts of New Zealand. We went through the videos of the individual players, in particular the new boys Lomu, Mehrtens, Glen Osborne at full-back and Josh Kronfeld, the No 7 openside flanker who had been one of the stars of the competition so far. We had not played against Kronfeld or encountered the juggernaut Lomu. There are distinctive traits which can be picked up with most players through watching enough video and this is what we were trying to achieve.

A couple of crocks - Neil Back and Dean Richards

Thursday, June 15th

ollowing the debacle yesterday at the Wanderers ground, we decided to revert
to our secret training venue which we used last week. The Spook had tried to
spy on the New Zealanders again today but the Kiwis were much more vigilant
than the Australians had been and he was unceremoniously turfed out, along with several other spectators. Clearly, everyone is wising up to the amount of spying going on.
Nobody is taking any chances.

We are now down to the final build-up and the main training sessions were taking a familiar theme: stretching, warming up with ball skills and what are called Auckland grids where
the squad is split into four equal groups which form the four corners of a large square. Various
running and passing drills are undertaken under pressure within this square. The main focus
today was on defence against the New Zealanders in what we anticipated would be a very
fast start by the All Blacks. In their earlier matches they had played a very wide game at great
pace and we needed to be able to reorganise our defence as they switched play from side to
side. As a back line, it was also important to get up quickly on their midfield, in particular
their wingers, especially if we were to have any chance of stopping Lomu. In the past couple
of years most of us had experienced two wins and two defeats against the All Blacks (two
defeats and a win by the Lions and one victory by England at Twickenham). Both these wins
had been based very much on solid and hardworking defence, and the taking of opportunist
tries, as scored by Rory Underwood in Wellington in 1993 when Sean Fitzpatrick lost the ball
on attack, much the same way as Lynagh had last week. We were confident that if our defence
held up, and we were able to cause them to turn the ball over, we would be left with a number of scoring opportunities. All of this, however, would stem from excellent, first-time tackling and not allowing the All Blacks to cross the gain line. In the two previous wins, I don't
think anybody missed a first-time tackle and we were exhausted at the end of it. We knew
what it would take to beat this All Black team and we worked consistently on the reserves
trying to imitate the New Zealanders and testing our defence to the limit. It's one thing to work
on your organisation to make it look good in practice. It's another thing doing it on the day
when it really comes down to one-on-one marking and tackling.

There had been a discussion between Jack and the senior players about changing the right
winger and putting Ian Hunter, a much bigger and stronger player, in to mark Lomu, or
whether Tony Underwood would be able to cope. We felt it best to stick with Tony, not least
because he has never let England down defensively, but also because of his superior pace.
I'm not sure Ian would have scored the try that Tony had last week against Australia and his
sheer pace could be vital.

While carrying out the first phase of our defensive operation in training I managed to go
over on my ankle rather badly which resulted in me leaving the training field to be put under
the careful observation of Smurf. It was one of those unfortunate incidents when nobody else
was involved, so that was it for today. Smurf was pretty confident that I wouldn't have a problem and he immediately got the magic ice out, but it meant that I couldn't do any kicking at
the end of the session. The afternoon was spent resting and having treatment in the hope that
tomorrow I can take part in the full session. We have been very lucky with injuries on this

tour, bearing in mind the physical intensity of the matches we have been playing. Going into the New Zealand game we are able to pick from the full squad of 26, all fully fit and raring to go.

As this was our second day back in Jo'burg, you can imagine that the press were keen for as many interviews as possible. I had spoken yesterday to Sara who had been inundated back home by the press which she found rather disconcerting. Arriving home from school with Emily she had found reporters and TV crews on the doorstep. She has been around long enough to cope, although even she found this intrusive. In fact, she reckons she has given more interviews than I have this week. Everyone was keen to get her thoughts on the coming game against New Zealand and they wanted to sit and watch the game with her. This was the last thing she wanted! As far as the press were concerned, things were really livening up in our hotel. Much of this afternoon was taken up with interviews. Chris Rea wanted a chat for a piece in the *Independent on Sunday* about the goalkicking and the drop kick in particular. He was focussing, quite rightly, on the kick five minutes before time which kept us in the competition. My old rival Stuart Barnes, now the *Daily Telegraph* rugby correspondent, also wanted a chat - the first time he had done a piece on me. There was quite a lot of amusement among the squad as they saw Stuart and I being pictured by the *Telegraph* photographer. After all the years in which we have been competitors, it will be interesting to see what Stuart writes about me. I'm sure he'll find it just as interesting. Jim Rosenthal even wanted to do an interview with Rory and myself talking about our schoolboy days for Tyne Tees TV. Clearly things were going mad back home and we were being treated as heroes, although, as with all media, they can be very fickle. As I keep maintaining, you're only as good as your next game, not the last one. And our next game is against the might of the All Blacks. The mental approach among the players was starting to build, particularly in the forwards, and we had recovered well from last Sunday. Mentally, we were back on line.

This evening's entertainment is being organised by The Judge who earlier had awarded the

'Dick of The Day' award to the manager for being too tense in the build-up to the New Zealand game. Any excuse, however, to see the manager wearing the cowboy shirt and gun holster meant there was never any doubt on the clapometer. We were now· in the Sandton Holiday Inn in a more upmarket suburb of Johannesburg and The Judge decided we would pop out for the evening to the local pizza restaurant only to find that tomorrow is a bank holiday in South Africa and the place was packed to the rafters with families eating out. We were hassled all evening by supporters wanting autographs and there was every chance the 'Dick of The Day' award tomorrow will be self-awarded by The Judge, who was not too popular.

Ian Hunter: we discussed putting him in against Jonah Lomu.

Friday, June 16th

More travelling again today as we move back to Cape Town this afternoon, which meant a bit of a rushed morning. After an early call and a quick breakfast, I was doing my Radio Five interview with Eddie Mair which had to be recorded to go out at 1.15pm.

The news this morning was two-fold. Firstly, several of the tabloids had run a story that I had decided to quit after the World Cup following, believe it or not, an article in the *Harrow Observer*, the Wasps' local paper, which attributed this gem of information to our Liaison Officer John Gasson. *The Sun* and *Daily Mail* had decided that a story in such an august journal as the *Harrow Observer* was one they should run nationally without checking it out with me. To put the record straight, I immediately refuted the story on the radio. Unfortunately, there is little you can do about such stories if reporters want to write them. I would be nice, though, if they bothered to check the facts, but perhaps that's asking too much of some of our media friends. The truth is never quite so exciting. Still, I thought I would give John Gasson a quick ring to give him a bit of stick. As expected, he also refuted any knowledge of it, although he did say he had spoken off the record with one of the *Harrow Observer* journalists months ago when they had discussed that one of the options for me after the World Cup was to retire. John promised to give the reporter a call and tell him to check out his facts in the future. I always find it funny that an off-the-record comment, of no real relevance, can reappear three months later on the eve of the World Cup semi-final when it might make a good headline. There was no harm done as far as I was concerned and as always I find these things quite amusing.

After training, carried out with my ankle heavily strapped, the second bit of news leaked to the press was the fact that I had been awarded the MBE in the Queen's birthday honours. I knew about this several weeks before we left the UK for the World Cup but I was not able to tell anybody. The press had been notified 12 hours before the announcement became public knowledge at midnight today. Terry Cooper, of the Press Association, was waiting at the hotel and was keen to get a comment from me. The last thing I wanted to do was to discuss my MBE just two days before the semi-final, although, of course, I was delighted and honoured to receive such an award. I did not want this to overshadow anything that was going to happen in the next 24 hours. Bearing in mind what had happened last Sunday, I thought there had been more than enough attention devoted to me. I just wanted to keep my head down and get on with the job in hand, so I had to spend the next hour before leaving for the airport trying to dodge the media or making bland statements like how much I was looking forward to next Sunday. The snappers were also out in force and had this great idea I should be pictured with a Union Jack over the top of my head. I politely declined as I have had experience of such things returning to haunt me at a later date. I had been caught out once or twice early in my career by the tabloids with a few set-up photographs only to wish I had never taken part. There were much more important things on my mind and I was glad when we got away from the hotel.

The training this morning was held again at the secret police ground and for once the South African sun was not baking down on us in the High Veldt. It had been eclipsed by a bank of low, grey cloud and a freezing north-easterly wind which reminded me of playing at Redcar on Boxing Day with the wind whipping in off the North Sea. It was absolutely freezing and it certainly made the players get on with training. We had another good session, effectively our final one for tomorrow's in Cape Town will be a very gentle run out. We knew we were good enough. It was just a question of who was big enough on the day to cope with the pressures and who would produce the big performance. The RFU President, Dennis Easby, who came to watch a lot of our training sessions, lent a hand today with my kicking session and, at 70 years-old, kept warm running around collecting my balls. I was delighted with Dennis' assistance, and I think he enjoyed the opportunity to keep warm.

Today was the South African premiere of the film 'Dumb and Dumber' and some of the boys were hoping to see this at the cinema once we got down to Cape Town. Many of them were keen to spend time at the cinema in the last couple of days before a game to fill in the long evenings after dinner. Unfortunately, they could not get in to see 'Dumb and Dumber' so 'The Bad Boys' was chosen as a poor substitute. I prefer to stay in the hotel watching rugby videos or playing table tennis or pool in the team room. The Australians stayed in this hotel before us, as they did before our victory over them at Newlands, so the omens were looking good. One or two people were starting to say that perhaps our name was on the Webb Ellis Trophy. I never believe in this type of talk, but I have played in games where fate plays a part and it may be, because of what had happened in the last five minutes against Australia, that we were definitely fated to win that game. I much prefer to believe in getting what you deserve, however.

Playing table tennis and pool in the team room is a much safer pastime than getting involved in the card school, although playing doubles against Victor Ubogu and Steve Ojomoh with Richard, our masseur, was an interesting challenge but one which we overcame, much to the chagrin of 'The Brothers'.

Ben Clarke putting his best foot forward in recovery training,
supervised by Dave Alred.

Saturday, June 17th

The news of my MBE had not really broken to the squad yesterday, but it was now official and was even in the South African newspapers this morning. So at breakfast I was once again the butt of their jokes, but I was quite happy to let them have their giggle, particularly if it helped relieve some of the tension. I was obviously very pleased with the news and Sara was inundated once again for her comments. It has certainly been some week - but I am more concerned about what will happen tomorrow.

Colin Herridge thought there was no way I could escape the TV guys out here. Rob Bonnet, from the BBC, and Sky's Jeremy Thompson, were keen to do interviews, so to get them off my back for the rest of the day it was decided I should have a word with them before our final team session at Newlands. It had been raining every day this week in Cape Town and the ground was much softer than it was against the Aussies last Sunday. However, this morning there was a glorious blue sky and here we are again training in perfect conditions, although the ground is a little soft under foot. I was caught out by the oldest trick in the book. Just as we started training, Will slapped me on the back and said "Come on, let's have a good session", only for me to find out afterwards that he had stuck a piece of paper saying MBE on my back. This then became the focus of attention for the rest of the squad and the TV crews with pictures beamed back home without me being aware of what was going on. Oh well, if it keeps everyone happy!

The mood was good in training and I could tell we were ready. We just ran through a few scrums and line-outs as a team, mainly at 50 per cent pace, to feel comfortable with the patterns we are playing, while keeping a few things up our sleeves as this final session is well watched by the media and spies from the enemy camp. They won't learn very much from our sessions the day before a game. The All Blacks had travelled down yesterday and this would be their first game a sea level, not that this would cause any problems. Many observers had suggested that a soft pitch, and even a wet day, would suit England better than the All Blacks and for once I did not disagree, bearing in mind the pace and skill level they had shown in their four games so far. After training I started a kicking session but ran out of time as the All Blacks arrived on the pitch for their training session. Dave and I decided we would return after lunch for a second session. I wasn't very happy with my goalkicking and was having a few problems with the non-kicking foot. The All Blacks did not hang about that long and I was able to have a good hour with no pressure to get my rhythm back. By the end I was feeling a lot happier and hoped tomorrow would not be a repeat of last week's dramatic last few minutes. Surely lightening could not strike twice?

The other semi-final, between South Africa and France, was due to kick-off at 3pm in Durban but we had heard on the radio that the game was in doubt because a deluge this morning had flooded the ground. Durban had been hit by a massive thunder storm. Not only were they worried by the flooding but by lightening striking while the game was on. This was a dreadful dilemma for the players who had arrived mentally prepared for the 3pm kick-off. By the time we got back to the hotel it had been decided that kick-off would be at 4.30pm. Derek Bevan had decided the pitch was playable after some concentrated mopping up and brushing by an army of volunteers. It was still raining when they kicked-off and one more sudden downpour in the first-half and it was quite possible for South Africa to go out of the World Cup because of their inferior disciplinary record, having had a player sent off against Canada. If the match had been abandoned in the first half, with neither side scoring a try, the only way a decision could be taken on who would go into the final would be on disciplinary grounds. If the game went into the second half and was then abandoned, the score at the time of abandonment would have stood. There were one or two uncharitable souls in the England camp praying for another cloud burst to see South Africa out of the cup. I think there would have been riots in South Africa if that had happened. The conditions completely dominated the game and it must have been a huge disappointment for both sides to play such a show-piece game in such conditions. The South Africans just about deserved to win through the superior play of their forwards and once again the good decision-making at half back by Joost van der Westhuizen and Joel Stransky. With the score at 19-15 to South Africa, and time rapidly running out, a five-yard burst by Benazzi finished only six inches short of what would have been the winning score. Derek Bevan was the toast of South Africa by not giving the try and, although there was some dispute from the French, video replay proved him to be right. Once again the French had left it late and had come close to knocking out the host nation. Nothing could dampen the spirits of the Natal faithful and the Springbok team which had achieved their goal of reaching the final of their first World Cup on home soil.

There were different views in the England squad as to who we wanted to get to the final, assuming, of course, that we would be joining them. Some wanted the South Africans to win so we would have the benefit of a huge occasion next Saturday with the host country playing at home. Others were rooting for France so there could be an all Northern Hemisphere final being staged in the Southern Hemisphere, which would do much to boost the game in our part of the world. We did not want a Southern Hemisphere winner yet again. Still, we now knew we would have to meet South Africa next week if we could overcome the All Blacks. We had always known that to win the World Cup we would have to beat South Africa, Australia and New Zealand. Some achievement!

The evening meeting was again taken by The Spook who had asked us this morning to think about what we were going to do personally to ensure success tomorrow. We then sat down as a squad of 26 to make our comments and there were some moving words spoken by all of the players, including the five who were not be involved in the match 21. They had all managed to get a game in the Pool matches but it was unlikely they would play again. However, they were all making a massive contribution to training and team meetings and they were just as much part of the squad as those taking the field. I sensed we were on the verge of something very big and one or two players were close to tears when we finished the meeting. Austin also reminded us of the comments we made about each other before the Australian game were still valid, stressing the value of looking over those comments to remind ourselves of what our team mates felt about us. We had often been criticised in the past for not being able to raise our game two weeks running after a big win. This had been the case on several occasions in the past, notably the British Lions' 93 tour of New Zealand when we won the second test but failed in the third, and also last year here in South Africa. But this week I felt all the preparations, both mentally and physical, had gone really well, and although we were very drained after the Australian match, it appeared to me we had overcome this. There was very little more we could have done and it was all down to the 80 minutes tomorrow afternoon to decide who would meet South Africa in the 1995 World Cup final.

England v New Zealand

Once again the skies were blue as I walked into the breakfast room, with the harbour clearly visible from the balcony. It looked as though we were in for another one of those beautiful Cape Town days.

The groundsman was now fully on our side and he allowed us back at 9.30 am to finish our kicking practice. We went through the usual routines, but I did not feel I was striking the ball so well as in the earlier parts of the competition. On leaving Newlands, many supporters were already browsing around the traders' stalls which circle the stadium. It was more like a scene from Pettycoat Lane than an international rugby venue, and a big crowd, possibly a sell-out, was expected. We had heard New Zealand were expecting huge support and there is obviously going to be a great atmosphere for this afternoon's semi-final. As we drove away from the ground we passed the Newlands Holiday Inn, where the All Blacks are staying, and their pack were doing their last-minute practicing in the car park. We asked the driver to surreptitiously pull over to have a quick spy on them for five minutes and it was clear they were going to throw the ball to the back of the line-out to Mike Brewer with Ian Jones peeling round the back, or throw the ball over the top to Josh Kronfeld. They were also practicing two and three-man line-outs to mix it up. From what we had seen in the matches so far, we had already picked out that this was what they had intended to do in any case. Nevertheless, it was useful conformation which we passed onto Brian when we got back to the hotel where our own forwards were about to start their car park exercise. This is all part of habit and helps to calm the nerves.

The backs' meeting at 11 o'clock focused on aggressive defence to make sure we did not let the New Zealand backs run. If they do, we are in trouble. We also wanted to capitalise on any mistakes they might make and maximise our own good play, as we had against the Aussies last Sunday with a try that came from good pressurised defence, forcing the Australians to make a mistake. We were confident we would get plenty of opportunities this afternoon and also had to make sure we stopped the New Zealanders in their tracks.

I spoke briefly to Sara who was going to the Petersham Hotel in Richmond to watch the game with the rest of the girls at the invitation of one of the national newspapers. I think she will be glad when all this is over and life can return to normality.

At the full squad meeting Jack played some video clips of our best play against the All Blacks as a last-minute confidence booster to reinforce the fact that we had beaten them and that if we played to our potential we had nothing to worry about. Often, many matches at this level are won on confidence and the collective belief of the team. The collective will of 15 players is what makes the difference. We had proved it before. We just have to do it again.

We were greeted on our arrival at Newlands by the Barmy Army, who had been very well behaved throughout the tournament and had given us magnificent support. We would certainly need this again today and I felt very proud as I walked into the entrance of Newlands. The ground was filling up and the atmosphere building as myself and Phil de Glanville went through our warming up and stretching exercises before doing some kicking at one end of the ground. One of the pleasures of playing the All Blacks, if you can call it that, is the facing up to the Haka, the traditional Maori war dance performed by New Zealand teams wherever they go. It's one of the features of international rugby and very much part of their culture. Over the years sides have attempted different ways of reacting to the Haka, which is clearly a powerful motivating weapon just before kick-off. Some ignore it altogether, as we did in the 1991 World Cup, as we stood in a huddle. Others take up the challenge by standing as close as possible to the New Zealanders. Several years ago the Irish team, led by Willie Anderson, virtually charged the Haka as they lined up, arms linked, ten yards away and walked slowly towards the All Blacks. They were virtually nose to nose by the time the Haka had finished. I'm not sure this is the best way of dealing with it. They could well have incited trouble before the game started. Most sides, like us, decide to face up to it, facing your opposite number and treat the Haka with the respect it deserves but not let it intimidate you. It's important to try and use it as a motivating tool for your own team and having stood up to the Haka on many times now, I don't think anyone in our side was in awe of this particular New Zealand team. It was clear, though, from the intensity of their actions that they were pumped up for this game and Mike Brewer and Jonah Lomu in particularly seemed to be performing it with additional fervour.

Unfortunately, as is confined to history, our World Cup campaign came to a sad end in Cape Town. In reality, it came to an end by about 3.10pm on this particularly Sunday. The All Blacks started with an intensity and pace the like of which I have never been on the receiving end of before at international level. We knew they would start quickly and move the game around. Although we were ready for this, I don't think any of us expected the onslaught which was to follow after the National Anthems were out of the way. Having won the toss, they chose to kick-off and immediately changed tactics by lining up the forwards on the right-hand side and decided to kick left to Jonoh Lomu on his own to get him into the game early. From that moment they seized the initiative from us and within minutes they had scored two tries and we were 12-0 down. The deficit was not necessarily critical in international rugby terms but the nature of the way the points were scored did cause some physcological damage. We had said all along that our first-time tackling would be the key but unfortunately missed tackles in the first five minutes cost us both tries as Jonah Lomu went in for the first of his four. Josh Kronfeld finished a sweeping move from their own 22 which came from the kick-off after the first try. We were clearly shellshocked by this storming start and never really recovered in the first half. By the interval we were trailing 25-3 and would need to perform miracles in the second half to get back into the game. Certainly we would need to score early and first but the All Blacks ran in two more tries early in the second half to take their tally to 35-3. We were staring an embarrassment in the face and the only thing left to play for was pride. After so much hard work our hopes had gone up in flames. We battled hard and, although pretty irrelevant, we did actually win the last 20 minutes by 26 points to 10. Maybe if we had been allowed to play for another hour we would have clawed back the difference. It was all desperately disappointing after our hopes had been raised so high last week with the win over the Australians.

It's always difficult to analyse a game blown apart in the first ten minutes because of the affect this has on both teams. Our missed tackles in the first five minutes effectively cost us the game. From then on we spent most of the first half trying to recover and the shock of those first few minutes clearly affected a lot of players and we started to make some elementary handling errors. I also failed with my first two kicks at goal and also a drop-goal attempt when we were trying to get some points on the board. Those misses were important as they may have helped to calm the whole team down. By the time we had sorted ourselves out the game was lost and we never had the chance to impose our game on the All Blacks. The skill level they showed in the opening 20 minutes was of a very high order and their new game plan was obviously based on getting the ball out wide to Jonah Lomu, who was well supported by a good set of three-quarters, particularly the two centres, Walter Little and Frank Bunce, the pace of full-back Glen Osborne, a quick back row and one of the best forwards in the competition, Josh Kronfeld, who was very quick over the ground. Their support play is also a feature of New Zealand rugby and they were very quick to get to the breakdown and recycle the ball. Historically, New Zealand rugby has always been based on their forward domination and eventually using the backs when the forwards had done the damage. They had moved away slightly from this, possibly because of the threat from rugby league and the desire to make rugby even more attractive. But they have also unearthed some extremely talented young players who like to have the ball in their hands. That's not to say they have lost the forwards' skills required at international level. In fact, without this their new game would not be possible and their scrummaging and line-out work is still of the highest order, although is does help when you have a 6ft 5in, 19 stone winger who we found impossible to stop. Nobody would ever point fingers in the England squad at players making mistakes, as nobody makes them on purpose, but clearly we had missed tackles in those first five minutes which shattered our dream. We scored four very good tries in the second half when we finally put together some quality rugby to show the rest of the world just what we are capable of. At least this meant we could leave the field with some of our pride restored.

It was a very distressed dressing room in stark contrast to the scenes only seven days ago in this same stadium.They say a week is a long time in politics. Well, I can assure you it is certainly a long time in sport. I have had my fair share of ups and downs in the last ten years of international rugby but I don't think I have experienced such a swing of emotions in the space of seven days. It was not just a case of desperate disappointment which I have experienced in close matches, such as the last World Cup final or the Grand Slam game against Scotland in 1990. This was more a disappointment borne out of shock, knowing we were never in the game. We ruined four years of hard work in only ten minutes this afternoon. That is the cruel world of international sport, and no doubt the Aussies had had similar feelings last week when we snatched victory in such dramatic circumstances. The French had also benefited from a last-gasp victory over Scotland, committing the Scots to a game against the mighty All Blacks in the quarter-finals, while in the semi-final yesterday they were on the receiving end when another last-gasp effort just failed. As Jack Rowell said in the press conference, it was the sort of game we would love to play again just to see if we could make a proper go at it this time. I certainly felt it was a nightmare from which I was about to wake from, that it hadn't happened and we could get on and do the job properly now. The sudden realisation that you cannot have another go is all too depressing.

'If only' are the two most useless words ever uttered by sportsmen after a defeat but no matter how useless they are we still keep using them. For the rest of my days they will be used a lot when we talk about our semi-final defeat by the All Blacks. If only we had won the toss and chosen to kick-off and thereby not allowing them to have the initiative. If only Will and Tony had not collided from the kick-off we may have scored from the other end. If only Jerry Guscott had nailed Walter Little in his 22 when he was clearing up a bad ball from Graham Bachop maybe we would have equalised. If only I had kicked my first drop-goal and two penalty attempts to keep in touch. If only. If only. If only...but then I suppose that when Zinzan Brook drops a goal from 45 yards it makes you wonder whether we were ever destined to win this game. Does fate play a part?

Unfortunately, we had to fly back to Johannesburg immediately after the game, another great decision from the World Cup organisers. So I had to put together my *Times'* interview with David Hands rather hurriedly outside the dressing room at Newlands. I don't like doing articles immediately after the game. I always prefer doing them the following morning when I have had a bit more time to reflect on what has happened and the reasons for it. Unfortunately, with us playing on a Sunday and the copy required for Monday morning, we had to do it there and then. I was careful to make sure I did not over react after such a defeat. I also had a quick word with Ricky Rothwell who was still here from last week. He could not believe we were flying out of Cape Town within the next hour. He had teamed up with another mate from college, Peter Higgins, and they had been looking forward to another night of celebration at the Sports Cafe. The waterfront at Cape Town this weekend will not be quite such a happy place for the England supporters. Tonight it will the turn of the Kiwi fans.

You know when your luck is really out when you board the aircraft and find that your victors are seated in Business Class and we had the embarrassment of trooping past them to be seated in Economy Class at the back of the plane. It had not been our day and it was a pretty unhappy and depressed England squad which took off from Cape Town for the final time.

It takes Dewi Morris and Will Carling to bring Frank Bunce to heel.

Monday, June 19th

Depression was still hanging over the England squad as we met at 10.30am before our now familiar recovery session at the local gym. Jack tried to coax one or two comments out of the players but no-one was particularly interested in saying a great deal. It would need more time for us to come to terms with what happened yesterday. Tony made some moving comments about how sorry he was as he felt he had let the squad down in his head to head with Jonah Lomu. There will never be any question of apportioning blame but Tony clearly had a difficult afternoon and wanted to clear the air. There was no doubt we were all with him and would have to regroup before now having to play in the third and fourth play-off game on Thursday in Pretoria, the one match none of us wanted to be involved in.

If nothing else, my swimming has improved on this trip and once again everyone went through a routine of 30 minutes of continuous activity to get the knocks and bruises out from yesterday before playing another major international in three days. Not the best of preparations but the French were in the same boat.

After our recovery session we went by coach to Pretoria, only 40 minutes up the road from Johannesburg, to the familiar surroundings of the Holiday Inn Crown Plaza , our home last year before our epic first test victory over South Africa when we had done to them what the All Blacks had just done to us. I spent the afternoon relaxing by the pool, catching up on some work as the sudden realisation hit me that this time next week we would be back in England and thinking about going into the office. The defeat yesterday was certainly going to make the final week in South Africa more difficult than we anticipated after our victory over the Australians. It will take a big effort from everybody to make sure the wheels do not come off altogether.

Will, Deano, Brian, Rory and myself met with the Spook at six o'clock to discuss ways in which we could try and lift morale in time for Thursday. We all felt it important that the senior players made a massive contribution to quickly lift spirits. At the team meeting afterwards Jack talked about how the squad had moved on a long way since he took over 12 months ago. He felt we were beginning to create something special with our achievements over the past year. Although yesterday had been a huge disappointment to everybody, we must continue to look forward and build on the foundations already laid. There was an urgent need for us all to sort out our minds before the game against France. This was a big test of character but, understandably, the mood was still downcast.

Tuesday, June 20th

This morning's team meeting before training was positive with the mood improving overnight. This was the opportunity for the senior players to put forward their views on what we had to do against France on Thursday and Jack asked a few of us specifically what we thought we were facing. Most of us responded by saying that over the years we had become a very proud outfit with considerable success on the international stage. Intermingled with this there had still been some days of bitter disappointment, which nobody enjoyed, but we had always been good at bouncing back quickly to prove to ourselves as well as the rest of the world that there was some steel in this English team.

There was nothing we could do now to bring back the performance against the All Blacks but it would be a big boost to everybody if we could finish third and overcome our great rivals from across the Channel. Equally, we had not lost to France since 1988 and it had been a long time since we had lost two internationals in a row. We did not want this to happen. A lot of players had worked very hard over the years in the England squad and some of the newer members were only just finding out the harsh realities of international life when things do not always go to plan. However, we had done it before and we could do it again and it was time for this squad once again to show its true character.

We had a really good training session, ironically possibly one of the best of the whole competition with great focus on what had to be done on Thursday. It was also one of the most aggressive sessions. Maybe this was just players venting their frustration from Sunday and the mood we were in this morning we could have played France here and now. I only hope this will still be the case on Thursday. We had played France on many occasions and had worked out how to beat them. There was nothing wrong with our game plan, it was just a case of how we would carry it out. Everybody seemed to be looking forward to the game.

There were two changes made to the side. Steve Ojomoh would come in for the battered and bruised Dean Richards, who had spent most of the competition carrying one injury or another. And Ian Hunter came in on the right wing for Tony Underwood, who Jack felt deserved a rest after the traumas of Sunday.

Many of the French TV and newspaper reporters were staying in our hotel and having spent a year in Toulouse I tended to be their first port of call for any interviews required. The French had also picked their team and had announced Albert Cigagna, who I played with at Toulouse, was going to win his first cap for France at the age of 34. He had always been regarded as one of the best uncapped No 8's in France and had been called out as a replacement for Philippe Benetton who had broken his arm against Scotland. I was delighted he would be getting his first cap against England. The only problem is that my French had deteriorated significantly from three years ago and to try and do television interviews in a language you don't speak very well is not the easiest thing in the world. But it provided some fun for the rest of the squad.

In the evening we ventured out to an Italian restaurant, again organised by The Judge. This one, however, was much better and the mood was strong as we also hatched a plan to go back to Sun City again on Friday, a dead day as far as we were now concerned before the final on Saturday.

Wednesday, June 21st

When you have been away for nearly six weeks in a tournament that has taken so much out of you, both mentally and physically, it comes as a relief to approach the final training session. The last time we will go through Smurf's warm-up session. The last time we will go through Les' ball drills. The last time for a while that I will have to stay behind to put in those extra hours of kicking practice.

We were back on one of my favourite grounds, Loftus Versfeld, where on that historical day 12 months ago, in front of Nelson Mandela, we had completely outplayed the new South Africa, their first test following the elections, and it was another one of those magnificent sporting occasions I had the privilege to be taking part in. I scored 27 points in our 32-15 victory and these were happy memories as we walked through the main entrance. All the stadiums in South Africa are full of history and feeling, each one with huge aerial photographs and ground-level action shots depicting the former glories of each of the unions. Loftus is the spiritual home of Northern Transvaal, otherwise known as the Blue Bulls, where Naas Botha spent so many years playing. He is still involved in rugby here, running the players' pool for the Northern Transvaal Union and generally spending as much time as possible on the golf course, having become a millionaire out of our amateur game through playing in South Africa and Italy in the Northern Hemisphere winter. I had always wondered why so many of the Southern Hemisphere stars like Botha, Campese and Lynagh ventured to Italy during our winter. There must be something there that attracts them. It can't just be the pasta!

The playing surface at Loftus is one of the best around and I was looking forward to spending a bit more time doing some more kicking in this superb stadium. The training session was not one of our best as for some reason the players seemed on edge and getting at each other. I was not too worried about this as it had often been the case on the day before a big game when one or two are a bit tetchy due to nerves. I take these nervy sessions to be a good sign because it means the players are concentrating. I got my rhythm back in the goalkicking and felt much better than I had done last week. The conditions might have had something to do with this: perfect under foot, perfect in the air with the ball travelling much further up here in altitude. No wonder Naas Botha kicked so many points for South Africa and Northern Transvaal in these conditions, some of the best anywhere in the world.

I spent the afternoon relaxing by the pool again with Rory and Will, discussing life and putting the rugby world to rights, as we often do. There are a lot of issues to be covered when we get back to England and as with a lot of players, we feel the game is at a crossroads as far as professionalism is concerned and the way the game is structured in the Northern Hemisphere. There is no question that the Southern Hemisphere is moving ahead. We know there is going to be an announcement in the next day or two about a new structure involving the big three - Australia, New Zealand and South Africa - playing each other home and away every year. I think our defeat against the New Zealanders last Sunday has brought home once again that the Northern Hemisphere is lagging behind in almost every aspect of the game, both on and off the field. For more than ten years Rory and I have been playing international rugby together and yet we were still frustrated by the fact that our administrators are always following rather than leading the other rugby nations. There does not seem to be anybody with the vision to take the game forward in a way to make England or our Northern Hemisphere colleagues the success story which we should be. Once again we are going to have a Southern Hemisphere champion in the third World Cup. We were still battling on in our old, amateurish ways while our cousins in the Southern Hemisphere were preparing the ground for a move towards professionalism which would take the game on to a new level over the next four years.

England and France have survived to a degree since the last World Cup and have registered one or two impressive victories, notably France's series victory in New Zealand last summer and our own series drawn in South Africa, but last Sunday showed once again that the Northern Hemisphere still lacks the environment in which the players can be tested against the best in the world. We had never been prepared for the kind of onslaught the New Zealanders threw at us as none of us play rugby at this intensity week in, week out. Maybe not even in the Five Nations championship, but certainly not in our league structure. The Southern Hemisphere have quality rugby just below test level in the Super Ten and their provincial matches. Although the Courage League has improved standards in England dramatically, it is too far removed from international standards to be of real value to the top players. As soon as you mention the creation of an elite in British sport, most of our administrators run a mile and are happy to carry on with mediocrity while the rest of the world moves forward, aiming purely to be the best and where success is something to be proud of. I can never understand this, bearing in mind how successful other aspects of British life are in terms of our business standing in the world. None of our business leaders are prepared to accept mediocrity and, in fact, they would not survive in this competitive world with such thoughts.

We could be helped greatly by our administrators sharing the same vision as the leading players of where we want English rugby to be. You often wonder whether there is the ambition to see English rugby at the top of the world ladder, or whether they are just happy to see us competing and finishing somewhere near the top. That's never been good enough for me, nor most of the players I have played with. We must strive to be better and we all agreed, reluctantly, that there was not anybody in our administration with the vision to take the game forward in England. There are so many vested interests in the structure of our game, from the counties down to the clubs, never mind the 56-man RFU committee. One thing we did agree on is that we should be playing Southern Hemisphere countries all the time. The focus of our attention should not be limited to the Five Nations, which, although a wonderful tournament, is no longer the be all and end all of international rugby. There is now a super league being formed by South Africa, Australia and New Zealand and it is imperative we are a part of this. If the gap gets too wide it will become increasingly difficult to close. Certainly by 1999 the gap could be quite substantial unless we are prepared to change our culture with regard to international rugby union in England. It is even more important that the idea of Club England becomes firmly established among the leading group of players, who will have to consider themselves first and foremost as English internationals who play for their clubs, rather than club players who happen to play for England. None of us were considering retiring just yet and we feel there are exciting times ahead, provided we take the threat from the Southern Hemisphere very seriously. Many discussions are taking place around the world on the way the game should be projected forward and we all agree that the next 12 months will see some far-reaching changes.

Having put the rugby world to rights, the rest of the afternoon was spent signing autographs and team photographs. Before leaving we had 750 caricature Five Nations prints to sign for charity but had not quite got through them all. So we got the company to send them out to South Africa so we could finish them off this week. There's always lots of signing sessions on trips such as this, especially near the end of the tour when both players' and supporters' charity organisations want mementoes to help raise money. Sometimes you can't get into the team room for a sea of rugby balls and other memorabilia waiting to be signed, but like everything else it all goes with the territory and is not too much of a hassle.

The evening team meeting was interrupted by a video of some ITV footage, not previously seen, dubbed over by Hale and Pace. This had been arranged surreptitiously by my roomy Rory and even featured Sara and Beth when they were in Durban. It was a well produced, light-hearted affair and

Graham Rowntree gets to grips with signing Five Nations caricature prints for charity.

starred Victor Ubogu posing as James Bond in a helicopter searching for Dennis Easby who was holed up in a five star hotel while the rest of the lads had to settle for a two-star Holiday Inn. Produced with the help of OD and Jim Rosenthal, it provided a comical interlude at our final team meeting. I had the feeling we were all looking forward to this final hurdle in our World Cup '95 campaign.

England v France

This is the day we dreaded from the beginning of the competition - matchday for the third and fourth play-off. The game we really never wanted to play. We have just failed at the worst stage to go out of the tournament, the World Cup semifinal, and we have to play another international three days later. In 1987 Wales played Australia and won the game to finish third in the world. In 1991 Scotland played New Zealand, with the All Blacks coming out on top. I hadn't met a single player in three World Cups who wanted to play in this play-off. It is purely there as another money spinner for Rugby World Cup with very little thought for the players. Funny that!

This year they had tried to make it a meaningful game by saying that for the 1999 World Cup only the top three plus the hosts, Wales, automatically qualify. Back in 1991 all eight quarter-finalists had been automatic qualifiers for 1995, but now the loser of this game would have to go through a qualifying group for the next World Cup. Therefore, we had to win this match as well as not wanting to lose to our old friends and rivals, the French, which would effectively mean losing the Northern Hemisphere title as well, having won a hard-fought Five Nations tournament. We desperately wanted to finish the tournament on a high after our disappointment last Sunday and had worked hard all week to lift the morale of the squad. The kick-off time was back to 5pm, more designed for television than the players, but also in the hope that the crowd numbers would be increased by people leaving work.

I decided to go down to the ground at midday for my usual morning of the game kicking session and also to meet up with Robert Louis Dreyfus, Chairman of the Adidas company, who was out for the weekend to watch the final. Being a Frenchman, he was looking forward to his countrymen gaining revenge over England this afternoon after eight years of consecutive defeats. I told him I hoped my boots would be responsible for the ninth consecutive defeat! Naas Botha, the king of Loftus Versfeld, was hosting the Adidas entourage and was also present while I was practicing my kicking. We had met briefly the previous year in the build-up to the first test and over the years he had noticed a significant change in my kicking style. Naas had been one of the greatest kickers of a rugby ball the world has ever seen and I had the privilege to play against him on the South African tour of England in 1992 just after they had been re-admitted to the sporting world. He was now retired, although there was talk just before the World Cup had started that he would be recalled to the South African side as they were worried about who they were going to play at fly-half. Naas had played in an invitation game for the late Danie Craven and press speculation had him coming back into the Springboks' side. But this did not materialise and he was happy now raising money for the North Transvaal players' fund. At the same time he had got his golf handicap down to one and was contemplating turning professional! I had many happy memories of this ground and was looking forward to our last match this evening.

The afternoon dragged and by the time we arrived at the ground the French were on the pitch doing their usual pre-match walk-around. The atmosphere was much more relaxed between the two teams as we mingled with the French players. I was particularly looking forward to playing against my old Toulouse team mates Albert Cigagna - his debut game - Christian Califano, the tighthead prop, and Emile Ntamack, one of the stars of the French team in this tournament. The other Toulouse player, Christophe Deylaud, had been left out of this game after what for him had been a disappointing tournament. Christophe had played at fly-half when I arrived in Toulouse but after some swapping around he settled in the centre and was capped in this position for France in 1992 before reverting to fly-half when I returned to England. It was a shame he was not playing today.

Unfortunately, this turned out to be one of our most disappointing performances for a very long time, even worse than the opening game against Argentina five weeks ago. Despite all the talk before hand, the boys were unable to raise their game before a large crowd of 40,000. We were very lethargic, slow to the ball and made lots of elementary mistakes. We played with a lack of fire and passion, unacceptable at this level. The French were not a lot better but showed one or two glimpses of their old selves. Although the game was quite close into the middle of the second half, they scored a couple of tries towards the end of the game to run out 19-9 winners, a satisfactory win for the French after their disappointments against us for so long but not a good end to the tournament for England. Franck Mesnel had been called back to fly-half and it was the first time he and Philippe Sella had won against England since 1988. Philippe Saint-Andre, the left-wing and captain, had never beaten us, so he was delighted at the after-match function that they had finally brought this depressing run to an end. And on top of this we have to go to Paris next season in the Five Nations championship! The only light relief was a brief chat with Ernie Els, the South African golfer who had returned from his tour of duty in the States to watch his countrymen in the World Cup final on Saturday. He had vowed at the start of the competition that if South Africa got to the final, he would return. Being a native of Northern Transvaal, he had popped in to see our game this evening. This was a sad end of Dewi Morris' career after he had had such an outstanding tournament. Still,

rugby players don't stay down too long and for the first time I can remember in all the years playing against France since 1985, the two teams had a night out together at one of Pretoria's most popular night spots - Ed's Diner. Despite a limited vocabulary on both sides, we managed to get on famously late into the night. Laurent Benezech, the Parisian prop, was heard to say: "It has taken me eight years to realise you English boys are not so bad after all." After the Five Nations matches there was little opportunity, and sometimes little desire, to mix with the opposition teams, particularly where there was a language problem, but here we had both finished our World Cup campaigns and Berbizier and his boys were in full swing, enjoying their victory. We decided on this occasion to adopt the maxim 'if you can't beat them, join them' .

The look on Martin Bayfield's face says it all after our last match defeat against France.

Friday, June 23rd

There were some sore heads on the team coach as we boarded for a nine o'clock departure to Sun City. The boys had taken a distinct liking to Sun City for the golf, water sports and gambling tables where several were hoping to win back the losses incurred on our previous visit. The two-hour journey provided the opportunity to sleep off the hangovers before our arrival before lunch. Unfortunately, this time the RFU were not paying for our stay, so we were not booked into the grandiose Palace Hotel but had to be content with the chalets in the Sun City Game Reserve.

A very pleasant outdoor lunch, overlooking the hippo park, was laid on for us and it wasn't long before the boys were disappearing in all directions to once again enjoy the facilities of this splendid resort. I caught up with the last few days of my diary and also a few more chapters of "A Long Walk To Freedom", although I admit defeat in not being able to finish Nelson Mandela's autobiography by the end of the tour. Goodness knows how long it will take me back home. I may still be at it when Christmas approaches.

Despite our defeat yesterday, and the fact that the squad is fairly tired and looking forward to going home, morale remained reasonably high and we were determined to enjoy our final evening in Sun City. We were treated to a barbecue by some of the members of staff, mostly rugby-mad ex-pats who were pleased to see us in their back-yard. They had had the pleasure of entertaining most of the visiting sides during the tournament and the barbecues were now down to a fine art. There will certainly be a few more sore heads on the way back to Pretoria tomorrow!

No, it's not the English forwards having lunch but our view of the hippo park at the Sun City Game Reserve.

Saturday, June 24th

Another two-hour coach journey after the second night on the beer within 24 hours rendered the art of meaningful conversation well and truly dead. In any case, we had probably talked ourselves out of meaningful conversation and it was a bit of an anti-climax waking up on World Cup final day knowing that all the excitement would be going on in the hotels of the two finalists. We might as well be a million miles away!

The squad was split 50-50 as to those who wanted to go to the final and those who preferred to watch it in the hotel, not being able to face the prospect of going to Ellis Park on a day that we all hoped we would be there ourselves. We had the World Cup closing dinner to attend in the evening, but the management, who had not been in Sun City, had decreed that although attendance at the dinner was compulsory, provided a decent number of players were willing to go to the final attendance would not be forced on those who did not want be there.

We arrived back at the Holiday Inn in Pretoria just in time for half of the squad to change and get ready to depart for Johannesburg. I had decided to watch the final on television in the hotel. I have never been a great watcher of live rugby matches, in any case, and always feel you get a better view on television, although obviously you miss the atmosphere. Even from the television, it was clear that the build-up to the game was something extra special, which we all expected as the South Africans had reached the final on their own turf and in their first ever World Cup. You could sense that although the New Zealanders, on form and on paper, had been the outstanding side during the competition, today could quite easily see an upset as the South Africans would be playing for their new nation. In typical fashion, Nelson Mandela was dressed in the No 6 Springbok shirt of captain Francois Pienaar as he was presented to both teams before kick-off. I don't think I know of any other world leader who would have graced such an occasion and made such an impact by choosing to wear the national shirt of South African rugby team which included the Africaaner Springbok emblem. The New Zealanders were not best pleased with this show of national pride by the President of South Africa and it was disappointing that one or two of them could not extend the courtesies with a little more warmth towards this great man. I know it is always tense before such a big game, and the presentations aren't the most important thing on the players' mind at that time, but in this instance some of the All Blacks clearly missed the point.

The whole ceremony, including the fly-past of the South African 747 which virtually touched the roof of the stadium, was quite spectacular. I don't think a low fly-past would have been allowed at Twickenham! However, it all added to the breathtaking atmosphere of the day and from the kick-off it was clear that not everything was going to go New Zealand's way. The first few minutes indicated that today may be different. For a start, the kick-off from Andrew Mehrtens, in which he attempted another unorthodox effort, did not go ten yards, thereby giving the South Africans a scrum back immediately, as opposed to going straight to Lomu, as in our match; the omens were definitely looking less favourable for New Zealand. One of the first times the New Zealanders tried to move the ball down the line, the ball went to ground and bounced behind Lomu instead of into his hands, as it had done the week before against us in Cape Town. The All Blacks started the game at the same pace as against England but in the first 20 minutes today they did not get the breaks and, in fact, were making uncharacteristic mistakes. Much of this was caused by phenomenal South African defence, especially every time Lomu got the ball. He did make one or two inroads into the South African line but on the whole he was extremely well marshalled. The stadium erupted every time he was tackled and the national 'Get-Lomu campaign' was seemingly working. James Small and his fellow backs, Japi Mulder and Joost van der Westhuizen, were all pulling off great tackles on the big man, and every now and again the back row of Pienaar, Mark Andrews and Ruben Kruger, also gave young Jonah a bit of a roughing up. This seemed to affect his confidence, which I am sure was part of the South African game plan. New Zealand were clearly under more pressure than they had been by any other side in the competition. Despite total dominance of the line-outs by Ian Jones, they persisted with their new running game and perhaps a slight change in tactics would have served them better. The match became a kicking game between Andrew Mehrtens and Joel Stransky, not only in terms of scoring points but also in some phenomenal touch kicking which, assisted by altitude, sent the ball 60 or 70 metres every time down the touchline, or the ball would be kicked dead from halfway or beyond if there were not other options. This was a favourite ploy of Joubert and perhaps one area where the law makers could make a sensible change to prevent a side kicking the ball dead. We all do it as part of a legitimate strategy for gaining territory but it has become monotonous and the problem is exacerbated at altitude where the ball travels huge distances with very little effort. Lomu was nearly set free with one very marginal forward pass decision when he could have clearly gone 70 yards to score, the one try needed by the All Blacks which would have probably won them the game. They persevered with their tactics, much as we had done against Australia in 1991, in the misguided hope that all was needed was one breakthrough and one try and the World Cup would be theirs. Unfortunately, as for us in 1991, this never came and a couple of missed drop-goal attempts by Mehrtens towards the end of the game took the match into extra-time, providing a tremendous climax for the two best teams in the competition. Joel Stransky's drop-goal with only a few minutes remaining was definitely the stuff of schoolboy dreams. I thought mine had been pretty good against the Aussies but to win the final with a drop-goal of this quality really was a fantastic achievement.

At the final whistle amazing scenes were witnessed at Ellis Park as the South African team dropped collectively to their knees as if in a prayer of thanks to God for what they had achieved. They had set out with the nation's hopes resting on them in that memorable opening game against Australia at Newlands and here they were world champions on home soil. As the game wore on I found myself compelled to the television. Although not a great game, it was a spectacular achievement for the South Africans and one which I was willing them on to as the game progressed. I still have no doubts that the New Zealanders were the best team in the competition but on this particular afternoon the South Africans played like men possessed and for their effort, determination and collective will to win they were, in my opinion, worthy winners of the Webb Ellis trophy. The presentation of the cup by Nelson Mandela to Francois Pienaar sparked off scenes of untold joy throughout South Africa. Mandela had inspired the nation during the whole of this rugby World Cup, from the moment of his opening address back in Cape Town to his presence here at the final to watch his Rainbow Nation clinch the mantle of world champions in their beloved sport. The streets around the stadium and in every major town and city in South Africa, erupted in celebration the likes that had never been seen before. Horns hooted, fans screamed with delight, flags were waving - all very similar to the Italians or Brazilians winning the soccer World Cup. I do now regret not being present in the stadium for such an occasion but this morning I did not feel able to spend my Saturday afternoon in the company of 60,000 South Africans. I think I missed out on a great day.

The evening end-of-tournament dinner was a bit of an anti-climax as these functions often are. We were kept waiting for the South African team to arrive, very much their prerogative as

The South African squad celebrate the World Cup final victory in the Ellis Park dressing room after their historic win over the All Blacks.

they had just won the World Cup. But we had not even had the main course when Louis Luyt, the President of the South African Rugby Union, rose to his feet to follow Sir Ewart Bell, who had presented the medals to the participating teams. He went on to make an infamous speech which brought down a sorry curtain on what had been an outstanding World Cup. In true Louis Luyt fashion he informed the rugby world that everyone was very fortunate to be in South Africa where the Webb Ellis trophy had been returned to where it belonged and the previous two winners, Australia and New Zealand, were lucky that South Africa had not been taking part in the previous two World Cups. We were clearly very lucky that they had been participating in this one. Not surprisingly, the New Zealanders were livid by such a speech and one or two had to be refrained from making their disgust known very forcibly to Mr Luyt. The New Zealanders did not hang around too long and before they departed we had managed to gather that much of the talk which had been going on in this week of the competition among the Southern Hemisphere countries and France had been about the possibility of a Packer-style rugby world conference organisation being put together. Most of the players we discussed it with were very keen on the idea. This was the first we had heard about it and we were informed that we would be contacted after our return to England. There was a lot of interest in this concept and we did not think this was the end of this particular issue. Before leaving I managed to talk to one or two of the South African players, including Joel Stransky and Hennie le Roux who were embarrassed by their President's comments. They were both very emotionally affected by their achievement and were in for a long night as we returned a little subdued to our base in Pretoria for one final night out with our French counterparts.

Sunday, June 25th

T he final day before departure always drags and although one or two of the players had gone off to play early-morning golf, the majority stayed around the hotel pool as well as finishing off the packing for the South African Airways ground crew who were coming to check us in mid-afternoon.

By now everyone was really on their last legs, especially after three late nights in a row, coming after five weeks of intense competition. There is not much of a bounce left around the England camp and most players would be quite willing to be transported in a time machine back to the UK and their family. A couple of lunchtime beers helped to raise flagging spirits for a short while before a late afternoon debriefing was organised by Jack and Will to get a few ideas before we dispersed, not to be reunited until September. Such meetings can be productive, but with so many tired limbs and minds not much was achieved. The general consensus was that we were disappointed with our five weeks' work, having come with such high hopes and that to maintain our competitiveness at such a high level it would need even harder work from all the squad, as well as a change in attitude towards the way we play the game in the Northern Hemisphere (despite the playing conditions we have to put up with) with more of a move towards the New Zealand type of game. This would not be easy given the quality and style of the week-in, week-out rugby in the UK. It was also agreed that Jack should go back to the UK and strive for more fixtures with our Southern Hemisphere cousins. It was ridiculous that we had not played the Australians for four years between World Cups. This was totally unsatisfactory and needed to be resolved.

Before leaving for the airport there was still time to fill and Jack and I sat over a cup of tea in the hotel lounge while the early-evening drinking school had already started in the bar. I had not sat down with Jack on a one-to-one basis very often and we managed to discuss a whole range of topics, all allied towards England being successful. I still felt that some players had to make a slight cultural change in their approach to training and all-out commitment to being successful at this level. World class international rugby is now at a pretty rarified level judging by the performances of New Zealand and South africa. If England are to maintain their position with the big boys, we will have to move forward. We had made great strides in the past five years, and improved enormously since the last World Cup, but as we have always said, the Southern Hemisphere lead the way in every respect and would continue to do so. We cannot rest on our laurels. If we do, we will be left well behind before the next World Cup. Professionalism has arrived and the 1995 World Cup will be seen as a watershed. Unless the players and administrators in the Northern Hemisphere are prepared to move forward on a united and radical front, there will be little or no chance of the winner of the 1999 World Cup coming from the Northern Hemisphere.

Monday, June 26th

It did not seem long, with the help of a couple of sleeping pills from The Doc, before we were back at Heathrow and being met by our loved ones. Having not seen them for three weeks, it was great to see Sara, Emily and Beth and I was looking forward to returning to some form of normality.

As we posed for family photographs at the airport I was reminded that the dust from our exploits of the last five weeks may take some time to settle and then we have Mr Packer and discussions with the RFU to look forward to. Before we know where we are it will be September and a new season and the world champions to prepare for at Twickenham on November 18th. The merry-go-round continues!

The home country captains get their hands on the Webb Ellis trophy at last - Gavin Hastings, Terry Kingston, Will Carling and Mike Hall can only reflect on what might have been.

Statistics

POOL 1	P	W	L	D	Pts
S. Africa	3	3	0	0	9
Australia	3	2	1	0	7
Canada	3	1	2	0	5
Romania	3	0	3	0	3

Australia 18, S. Africa 27
Canada 34, Romania 3
S. Africa 21. Romania 8
Australia 27, Canada 11
Australia 42, Romania 3
Canada 0, S. Africa 20

POOL 3	P	W	L	D	Pts
N. Zealand	3	3	0	0	9
Ireland	3	2	1	0	7
Wales	3	1	2	0	5
Japan	3	0	3	0	3

Wales 57, Japan 10
N. Zealand 145, Japan 17
Ireland 50, Japan 28
N. Zealand 34, Wales 9
N. Zealand 43, Ireland 19
Ireland 24, Wales 23

POOL 2	P	W	J	D	Pts
England	3	3	0	0	9
W. Samoa	3	3	2	1	7
Italy	3	3	1	2	5
Argentina	3	0	3	0	3

W. Samoa 42, Italy 18
England 24, Argentina 18
W. Samoa 32, Argentina 26
England 27, Italy 20
Argentina 25, Italy 31
England 44, W. Samoa 22

POOL 4	P	W	L	D	Pts
France	3	3	0	0	9
Scotland	3	2	1	0	7
Tonga	3	1	2	0	5
Ivory Coast	3	0	3	0	3

Scotland 89, Ivory Coast 0
France 38, Tonga 10
France 54, Ivory Coast 18
Scotland 41, Tonga 5
Tonga 29, Ivory Coast 11
Scotland 19, France 22

KNOCK-OUT RESULTS

QUARTER-FINALS
South Africa 42 Western Samoa 14
France 36 Ireland 12
England 25 Australia 22
New Zealand 48 Scotland 30

SEMI-FINALS
South Africa 19 France 15
New Zealand 45 England 29

3RD/4TH PLAY-OFF
France 19 England 9

FINAL
South Africa 15 New Zealand 12

England Teams

Vs ARGENTINA, 27/9/95
Won 24-18
M Catt, T Underwood, W Carling (capt)
(rep P de Glanville 75 mins), J Guscott,
R Underwood, R Andrew, D Morris,
J Leonard, B Moore, V Ubogu,
M Johnson, M Bayfield, T Rodber,
B Clarke, S Ojomoh (rep N Back 34-37,
48-53 mins).
Scorers:
Pens: Andrew (6).
DG: Andrew (2).

Vs ITALY, 31/5/95
Won 27-21
M Catt, T Underwood, P de Glanville,
J Guscott, R Underwood, R Andrew
(capt), K Bracken, G Rowntree,
B Moore, J Leonard, M Johnson,
M Bayfield, T Rodber, N Back,
B Clarke.
Scorers:
Tries: T Underwood, R Underwood.
Con: Andrew.
Pens: Andrew (5).

Vs WESTERN SAMOA, 4/6/95
Won 44-22
J Callard, I Hunter, W Carling (capt)
(rep D Hopley 70 mins), P de Glanville,
R Underwood, M Catt, D Morris,
G Rowntree (rep J Mallett 25 mins),
G Dawe, V Ubogu, M Johnson, R West,
S Ojomoh, N Back (rep T Rodber 33
mins), D Richards (rep K Bracken 74
mins).
Scorers:
Tries: Underwood 2, Back, penalty try.
Cons: Callard (3).
Pens: Callard (5).
DG: Catt.

Vs AUSTRALIA, 11/6/95
Won 25-22
M Catt, T Underwood, W Carling (capt),
J Guscott, R Underwood, R Andrew,
D Morris, V Ubogu, B Moore,
J Leonard, M Johnson, M Bayfield,
B Clarke, T Rodber, D Richards.
Scorers:
Try: T Underwood.
Pens: Andrew (5).
Cons: Andrew.
DG: Andrew.

Vs NEW ZEALAND, 18/6/95
Lost 45-29
M Catt, T Underwood, W Carling (capt),
J Guscott, R Underwood, R Andrew,
D Morris, V Ubogu, B Moore,
J Leonard, M Johnson, M Bayfield,
B Clarke, T Rodber, D Richards.
Scorers:
Tries: R Underwood (2), Carling (2).
Cons: Andrew (3).
Pen: Andrew.

Vs France, 22/6/95
Lost 19-9
M Catt, I Hunter, W Carling (capt),
J Guscott, R Underwood, R Andrew,
D Morris, J Leonard, B Moore,
V Ubogu, M Johnson, M Bayfield,
T Rodber, S Ojomoh, B Clarke.
Scorers:
Pens: Andrew (3).